Routledge Revivals

Free Trade and the Empire

Free Trade and the Empire

A Study in Economics and Politics

by
Professor William Graham

Routledge
Taylor & Francis Group

First published in 1904 by Kegan Paul, Trench, Trübner & Co. Limited

This edition first published in 2019 by Routledge
2 Park Square, Milton Park, Abingdon, Oxon, OX14 4RN
and by Routledge
52 Vanderbilt Avenue, New York, NY 10017

Routledge is an imprint of the Taylor & Francis Group, an informa business

© 1904 by Taylor & Francis

Publisher's Note
The publisher has gone to great lengths to ensure the quality of this reprint but points out that some imperfections in the original copies may be apparent.

Disclaimer
The publisher has made every effort to trace copyright holders and welcomes correspondence from those they have been unable to contact.
A Library of Congress record exists under ISBN:

ISBN 13: 978-0-367-24606-8 (hbk)
ISBN 13: 978-0-367-24610-5 (pbk)
ISBN 13: 978-0-429-28344-4 (ebk)

Free Trade and the Empire

FREE TRADE AND THE EMPIRE

FREE TRADE

AND

THE EMPIRE

A STUDY IN ECONOMICS AND POLITICS

BY

PROFESSOR WILLIAM GRAHAM, M.A.

AUTHOR OF

'SOCIALISM NEW AND OLD,' 'ENGLISH POLITICAL PHILOSOPHY'

ETC.

LONDON

KEGAN PAUL, TRENCH, TRÜBNER & CO. LTD.

DRYDEN HOUSE, GERRARD STREET, W.

1904

PREFACE

THE chief object of this pamphlet is to set forth, in a connected form, the main aspects of the great tariff controversy now for some time before the public; to treat the question more deeply and fully than the exigencies of the platform usually allow; and at the same time to treat it, as far as may be, from a scientific and as little as possible from a party point of view.

The question is one both of economics and politics, and it raises the most important and delicate and complicated issues in both subjects. On the economical side I have treated the question from the point of view of the new Historical and Comparative School, as well as from that of the traditional or Deductive School from Adam Smith to Mill; believing, as I do, that the latter method alone is likely to shut out important aspects of the subject, and especially to hide the truth, which is the great lesson of the newer school, that economic doctrines are rarely of absolute or universal application, but are relative to time, country, and the circumstances of each country.

But the question is also political as well as economic, and political considerations cannot be dispensed with in the question of Free Trade and Protection; in regard to which great interests within a nation may be opposed to each other, while high interests of the State as a whole in relation to other States may be involved; it is also a political question so far as it is connected with the question of Imperial Federation, or closer union between the Mother Country and the Colonies; and in both respects the best political ideas of our time will be needed for the proper solution of it.

Above all, in dealing with a question involving the future of the United Kingdom as well as of the British Empire itself, it is necessary to rise above the merely party point of view, or the temporary interests of parties. What is needed is wider and clearer light, uncoloured by party, undistorted by sectarian bias or dogma. There is wanted an appeal from platform or press arguments equally confident—though contradictory to each other, and equally drawing on narrow principles and limited knowledge—to wider

principles, a more impartial tribunal, and scientific
methods that admit of some sort of verification ;
and the attempt is here made to furnish such
a fuller and more scientific treatment of the
question, while at the same time to make it as
intelligible as the difficult nature of the subject
admits.

There is, I believe, a large and intelligent
class wanting this further light and more exact
treatment, and it is to this class mainly that the
following pages are addressed in the hope that so
far as the policy advocated and the reasons urged
in its favour recommend themselves to their intelligence, it may, through their influence, have
some effect in the sphere of practice ; that it may
at least do some good or prevent some evil,
especially rash or premature action where retreat
might be difficult or impossible.

It may be well to add that the conclusions
reached in Chapters III, IV, and V were held
long before the present controversy was raised,
as may appear from the following passage written
by me in 1890, when dealing with the question of
Foreign Trade in its relation to English wages :—

The further cure for low wages, at least for
England, the circumstances of each country being
special, would consist not so much in emigration
or additional restraints on population as in the

discovery of new and free markets for our manufactures; the diminution or removal of hostile
tariffs by treaties or conventions, which where our
self-governing colonies are concerned might be
arranged between the Imperial and Colonial governments. . . .' ('Socialism, New and Old,' 1890).
In this sentence the reader will perceive the germ
of the chapters on Retaliation, Preferential Tariffs,
and Neutral Markets.   But what is there only in
germ is fully developed in the present pamphlet,
and what is there given as an opinion is here
supported by detailed arguments, and maintained
against the chief conflicting views.   Chapters
VI and VII are mainly devoted to a consideration of the ideas of Mr. Chamberlain on Protection, the self-sustaining Empire, and Imperial
Federation.

CONTENTS

FREE TRADE AND THE EMPIRE

CHAPTER I

FREE TRADE AND PROTECTION IN THE NINETEENTH CENTURY

I

DURING the first fifty years of the nineteenth century England enjoyed a monopoly in nearly all branches of manufacture, in addition to her commercial supremacy. The monopoly extended to the various textile industries of cotton, woollen, linen, lace, silk; the iron and steel industries; the hardware industry. She had her supremacy from the great series of new inventions which made the Industrial Revolution, which inventions enabled her to produce on a great scale and far more cheaply than before, and much more cheaply than the foreigners working with their ruder methods and apparatus. England enjoyed this

B

monopoly unchallenged during the Great War, and for some quarter of a century afterwards. During the war the old industries on the Continent were gradually broken up, though the old rude methods long survived. England supplied the Continent with manufactures so far as Napoleon's Berlin Decrees and exclusive policy allowed it.

After the war the Continental nations still more bought English manufactures—linen, woollen, cotton, hardware—and gave in return corn, wines, timber, wool, raw flax, hemp, etc. Duties were levied on imported goods on both sides, but they were not protective duties, except the English duties on corn ; for the Continental nations had scarcely any manufactures to protect or that competed with ours. England, having the monopoly of many industries, naturally enjoyed high prices and a very great rate of profits. The high prices were not the concomitants, as monopoly prices sometimes are, of a narrow market. There was a vast demand, almost a world-wide demand, for commodities, some of them being of the nature of necessaries : a demand so great that the supply could never overtake it, so great that the supply of the raw material of one of them—the cotton—was always short and that the wages of all the operatives in Lancashire were continually increasing. Even when the powers of production were greatly multiplied by the substitution of steam for water-power in factories and mills, the demand was still largely ahead of the supply.

It was a unique and unparalleled position that England enjoyed for half a century at least, during which period she laid the foundation of her wealth, which continued easily to increase afterwards and which is still greater than that of any other country save the United States. She had the start, the inventions and machinery, the skilled labourers. She alone possessed the great capital necessary for production on the great scale which enabled her to command the foreign market as well as her own.

But it was scarcely to be expected that Germany, France, and other advanced nations which formerly supplied their own manufactures, and whose artisans were fitted to supply them, should acquiesce in the new economic *régime* under which they were compelled by force of the universal demand to pay higher prices for goods than those at which they could themselves produce them. For that was the fact, as alleged by German economists, and it appears to be true from the economic situation in which one nation alone produced all manufactures for all other nations.

Moreover, German statesmen, publicists, and economists had to consider the social and political problem presented by distressed and idle hands deprived of the old occupation, with their growing-up children for whom the old industries were closed; perhaps one-third of the people had formerly depended on their manufacturing industries for a livelihood, and now their labour was no longer needed. What was to be done with them? The absolute Free Trader does not care to face the question. All these people could again be usefully employed in their own country in producing the imported manufactures, and at a price no higher than actually prevailed, if the Government would only put on such a duty as would place the English and the German manufacturer in a position of equality; because it was granted that the English producer had an advantage at first in capital, skilled labour, and established connection, so that his costs of production were less than the German producer's, and a duty which amounted to this difference was only fair to the latter. Otherwise there would have been no possibility of starting the manufactures and making a fair profit. The English producer could always sell cheaper, and with his wider margin of profit could well afford to do so, and for so long a time that the German manufacturer must perforce in the end be driven out, just as in the case of Trusts at the present time, which can always undersell outside competitors.

Had there been no attempts to restore the German manufactures all these unemployed people and their children would have had to devote themselves to the other callings, mainly agricultural, already fully manned, such as the production of corn, or wine, or timber, or tobacco, or flax, a work to which the grown labourers were untrained. Their other alternatives were public or private charity or emigration. And in all other countries where English manufactures had killed the home manufactures they would have been presented with the same alternatives. Had all such gone, indeed, in Germany and elsewhere, to various branches of agriculture, or wine making, or timber producing, etc., doubtless England would have got her food and raw materials and luxuries cheap, with all the world producing them for her. The situation would have been most favourable for England both ways. She would have manufactured for the world—would have been one vast workshop. But she had only a moderate population, a large part of which was engaged in agriculture; she could not supply the world without charging high prices, while all others selling a great supply in a small market would have had to lower theirs : 'to buy in the cheap market and sell in the dear,' Cobden's maxim of economic wisdom, would have been thus possible for England, but for her alone.

For the reasons just mentioned Germany adopted a policy of Protection, and for similar but stronger reasons she continues Protection, the abandonment of which would mean the speedy ruin of many of her industries, and the like holds of France and other countries. In Germany and France there is protection both for manufactures and, within the last few years, for agriculture ; for the former against England chiefly, for the latter against the United States chiefly, though it applies to other nations that can produce cheap corn, such as Canada and Argentina. The reasons for protecting agriculture are chiefly political : first the contentment of the agricultural population who form in both countries the bulk of the population ; secondly for a deeper reason, from the statesman's point of view—namely, to keep up the numbers of this interest, so important for a great military nation as the nursery of its best and most virile soldiers, which would certainly be diminished, as well as their prosperity endangered, by the admission of American wheat at prices 40 per cent. lower than the prices at which the German and French peasants could 'live and thrive.' Accordingly, Germany and France have put on duties and increased them to 7s. 7d. and 12s. 2d. per quarter in Germany and France respectively ; the safety of the State being here regarded as paramount in spite of the increased price of food.

There is no room here for the application of the theory of Mill and Ricardo—namely, that there should be a division of labour between Germany and England with respect to any two commodities producible by both of them, but at different costs of production (measured not in money, but hours or days of labour, which it would be impossible to calculate) ; that England should produce for both the commodity, say cloth, in which she has the greatest advantage, while Germany produced the linen for both ; that they should then exchange them at some rate determined by the comparative amount of their mutual demands, which would divide the advantages of the trade between them, and so that each should gain. I say there was no room for the application of such a theory when England, after the industrial revolution, had monopolised both the linen and the cloth—in fact, all the textile industries—and was not likely to suggest any such division of labour. England had the machinery ready in all, and was actually manufacturing all textile goods, and not only all the soft goods, but all the hardwares ; and if Germany had started any of them without protection, she would have been undoubtedly met by underselling. England (or rather, in this case, Ireland) could no doubt have dropped the linen industry to Germany and kept to the cotton and woollen, but she would have been very unlikely to do so, thereby losing much capital and acquired skill.

At any rate, she did not do so, nor could Germany ever have left all the manufactures to England while she took to the production for both, say, of corn, for there were high protective duties on corn in England up to 1846, while even when the corn duties were removed Germany had no chance in the English market with her corn in the face of American competition.

There was, therefore, no possible room for the application of Mill's theory of comparative cost between England and Germany, or England and France. It seemed to foreign statesmen and economists desirable to restore the old industries for which, except perhaps the silk industry, all three countries appeared equally suitable. But at first England had an advantage which could only be met by protection.

When Cobden preached free trade it was on no such inapplicable theory as Mill's. He adopted a much simpler and more efficacious method. Cobden was a manufacturer, and saw that if he could get his raw material cheap, and corn, the chief food of the labourers, cheap, the English could sell their manufactures cheaper than other nations.   He was mainly thinking of getting food and raw materials cheap ; hence he advocated the removal of duties.   His free trade had no deeper foundation than that.   Remove these barriers and we can undersell other people.   He never advanced a general argument on the subject, such as Mill's, and wisely.   He kept to what he could grasp : no tax on corn which would make bread dear ; no tax on materials which would make finished goods dear, and which would place us at a disadvantage with possible competitors who did not tax either.   This maxim specially suited England at the time, to admit all free—food, raw materials, and manufactures.   She had nothing to fear from the free admission of manufactures.   They were not likely to be many, and they would probably be non-competitive. But what suited England so well did not equally suit Germany or France, and they, as we have just seen, founded and fostered the industries in order to deliver themselves from the English monopolies of all manufacturing industries— by determining to produce a part at least for themselves, and perhaps for some other countries beyond the range of English commerce.

II

Thus far as regards Germany and France, whose economical circumstances were somewhat analogous, and where by means of protection their national industries temporarily destroyed were re-established, and where some new ones were created which were made possible by means of scientific discoveries.

The case of the United States is altogether different, and for the purpose of our inquiry is even more interesting and instructive, especially in showing that the question of Free Trade and Protection is a relative one, and cannot be profitably treated by abstract and general arguments irrespective of historical considerations as well as the special and actual circumstances of each country.

The United States forms the larger and richer half by far of a great continent. It is fully as large as Europe, with vast areas of fertile and virgin soil; with abundant gold and silver, and, still better, coal and iron; with oil springs to supply the world; and a varied but generally con-

genial climate for man, and favourable to the
growth of all kinds of natural products—cereals,
tobacco, raw cotton, and of all kinds of fruits and
vegetables. Besides arable land, it has immense
tracts of pasture land which support many
millions of cattle, sheep, and horses. · This land, so
favoured by nature, is peopled by eighty millions
of mixed, and particularly of British, origin, but
all tending to a peculiar human type, marked by
great energy and inventiveness ; a country where
the average man and the 'people' in general have
reached a higher level of intelligence than pre-
vails in any other civilised country. They form
the best workmen, as their directors are unrivalled
in resource and quick and apt to see and to
adopt new methods and devices. The latter are
more absorbed in their business, and devote to
it more time and thought and energy than the
industrial chiefs elsewhere ; while their original
inventors and discoverers, their Edisons and
Graham Bells, are second to none in their appli-
cations of the discoveries of science to the aid
of old industries or the creation of new ones.

The Americans had first to clear the forest
and prairie, and to drain the swamp ; and under
the stimulus of private ownership they did it so
effectively that within a century almost it was
cultivated from the Atlantic to the Pacific, and

from the Great Lakes to the Mexican Gulf. The colonists at first practised only the simple mechanical handicrafts and home manufactures. They made most of their tools and furniture, only the richer sort imported from England finer furniture and choicer articles or materials of dress; and so they continued in this simple style of life until the revolution precipitated by England's colonial policy and unwise taxation.

After their Independence was acknowledged in 1783 they still continued to depend on English manufactures, and even, as they grew richer, in a greater degree; all the more so as the industrial revolution was more and more giving England a monopoly as against the world for the next fifty years or more. It was not till the year 1825 that in a small way America started manufactures for herself, at which date she put her first duty of 25 per cent. *ad valorem* on English imported goods.

The Americans had prospered as farmers in the Eastern and New England States; they prospered still more as the Valley of the Mississippi and the West began to be cultivated, where light farming on virgin soil produced great crops for which, after the repeal of the Corn Laws, they had a ready and profitable market in England. They also exported timber and tobacco,

as well as raw cotton, from the Southern States.
They continued mainly an agricultural people,
but with an increasing commerce, internal and
external, and with a certain aptitude for building
fast-sailing ships. Their mining industries were
not yet begun.

Then came the gold discoveries of 1849–50
which drew many emigrants to California. The
question of free trade and protection was keenly
discussed about this time, and the American
statesmen favoured protection, both on political and economic grounds. It was maintained
that it was not good for a nation to have only a
few industries connected mainly with agriculture ;
that variety of industries, manufacturing and
commercial, as well as agricultural, was necessary
to call into exercise all the industrial capacities of
the people. Again, it was urged that manufactures were necessary to give employment to the
constantly increasing population, which could
not all find it in agriculture or in the crafts of
the ordinary artisans ; and, of course, the pro-
tectionists' argument so often since repeated
was employed, that it is desirable that a nation
be self-sufficing and independent of foreign
nations, and especially in a country so liberally
endowed by nature as America.

The first argument, which is known as the

'political argument,' has a good deal in its favour, especially in the peculiar case of America. A nation as a whole from the point of view of industrial and general progress requires more productive labourers than farmers, herdsmen and fishermen, even when supplemented by 'the mason, the shipwright, and the carpenter'; and the American, as since shown, had great natural aptitudes for manufactures, with all the technical processes involved, in their native intelligence, skill, and dexterity in handling tools, in tending and superintending machinery. It was believed further that, with the national advantages resident in the soil and people, with the raw materials, in the case of cotton, within the country, they could produce for themselves the important textile fabrics as easily as the Europeans and with as little expense of labour and capital.

A certain truth in the political argument we have allowed : variety of industries is desirable, but it does not follow that a nation should undertake *every* industry and import *no* manufactures, unless it is superior to every other nation in every branch of manufacture. And this is certainly not the case with respect to some of the textile industries, such as the cotton, linen, woollen, and silk. For it has been proved, after a great many years of experience, that in spite of their excellence as

operatives the Americans cannot successfully
compete with labourers of the United Kingdom
or the Continent in these industries. They still
require an *ad valorem* duty of from 40 to 50
per cent., the prices at which they can profitably
produce being so much higher than in England.

According to the American employers they
could compete on equal terms and could dispense
with the high duty but for the fact that they pay
50 per cent. higher wages than are paid in England (and 130 per cent. higher than in Germany).
They say, ' If we could reduce our wages to anything like the European level, or even the
English level, we could compete and sell at as
low a price ; but it is impossible to reduce the
wages, and we do not desire to do so, so that we
have no alternative but to call upon the State to
shelter us by such a tariff as will place us on an
equality with the English producer.'

There is something in this plea. But it is
not altogether satisfactory. For it is generally
believed, and it is asserted by American economists like Professor Walker, that the American
worker in general, if more highly paid, is superior
in efficiency in a still higher proportion, the work
done being so much greater in amount or quality
that it is actually profitable to give the higher
wages. I do not believe that this is generally

true of all industries, for if it were, the American cost of production would be no higher than the English (unless the employers expect higher profits in America), and the prices would have been no higher, so that there would have been no need for protection.   But it appears certain that their cost of production, and consequently paying prices, are higher.   Hence their cry for protection.

There is another reason why they cannot compete without the duties.   Originally the operatives in the textile trades in Lowell and Paterson were a superior class, and the duties were then really lower and possibly might have been dispensed with ; but since 1850 a vast and increasing stream of emigration from all countries of Europe (especially Great Britain and Ireland) set in, and a great number of these emigrants could not find employment on the land or in their own trades, some of whom and their children found employment in the mills and factories, while the older class of workers and their children gradually found better paid and higher employment, in a country ever starting fresh industries in the huge cities springing up all over the country.   So the sons and daughters of the emigrants took their places in the New England factories abandoned by the native-born Americans.   But the newcomers took time to learn the technique, and their labour was hence less valuable to the manufacturer, and so protection became still more necessary and was increased in 1861 by the Morell Tariff, and afterwards by the McKinley Tariff (1890), and the Dingley Tariff (1897).

The fact that they still require such high protective duties proves either that the industries should never have been started; or, at least, when the inferior operatives took the place of the better ones who left the industries, that the tariffs should not have been raised—that it should rather have been the policy of American statesmen not to encourage the industries by high tariffs, but gradually to lower them and allow English competition on more equal terms, so as not to attract fresh young labour to these industries, but to direct them rather to some more promising fields. And the statesman, had he done so, would have had on his side all the body of consumers who are taxed to keep unsuitable, or at least costly, industries in existence.

But this does not apply to the iron and steel industries, which were started at Pittsburg about 1870. These latter were reasonably sure of their future, but they required protection in their early days against the formidable ironmasters of the North of England. The great industry that is now one of the world's wonders, was an infant industry

c

in 1870, when the Pennsylvania ironmasters asked
and obtained from the Government considerable
protective duties that it could now dispense with
altogether as regards its best products and
qualities.   Abundant coal had also been found,
without which this result would not have been
possible.   Then petroleum oil was discovered
and natural gas.   Machinery and tools, in which
the Americans excel, were made, also watches
and clocks, boots, bicycles, sewing and type-
writing machines, leather, paper, etc.

It is now apparent that the remarkable people
of this fortunate land are in such a unique
position that they could supply within their own
bounds ample necessaries of all kinds, besides
conveniences, comforts, and most luxuries.   They
could cease all commercial intercourse with the
outside world and do very well.   They could be
nearly economically independent and self-sufficient, if that be the true ideal.

But, as a matter of fact, the farmers and
planters find it necessary to export to Europe
a vast amount of wheat, maize, raw cotton, and
tobacco; also cattle, oil, bacon, hams.   They produce more than is required in America; some of
the products are mainly for foreign consumption.
But besides these exports, amounting to 106
millions in 1902, they exported iron and steel,

boots and shoes, watches, and other manufactured
goods, to the value, last year, in manufactured
and partly manufactured goods, of 21 millions.
They exported all this to England.   They also
exported to a large extent to France, Germany,
and other countries; but they import comparatively little, because their self-sufficing theory
excludes most foreign manufactures, and they
require few necessaries except tea and sugar.
No doubt they import certain luxuries not producible in the happy Union—Champagne and
Johannisburg for the millionaires, costly silks
from Lyons for their wives, together with pictures
by Old and New Masters, Parisian articles of
taste, etc., and they owe our shipowners a pretty
sum for freights, and also investors on this side
the water, for dividends.   Still, in spite of all this
there is an increasing balance due in gold—of
little use once the needs of the currency are met—
to the nation as a whole (however great a
reserved purchasing power and command over
the world's goods it gives to wealthy owners of
it) ; of no use but so far as it gets into circulation
to raise prices, with all the injury thereby possible
to different classes, while if it does not get into
circulation and is not employed as capital, it is so
much barren metal.

   If the Americans had been but content to leave

to Europe or England some of the textile trades, they might have taken much of their favourable balance out in cotton, linen, woollen, silk, or lace goods, to the great relief of American consumers, and without any possible disturbance of the currency; while the American employer and operatives now in these industries would not have been injured, because they would have been engaged on some other more profitable ones.

III

The circumstances of England were, and are, wholly different. The Industrial Revolution, and the fact that she had the start with the new and potent means of production, that for a long time she had far more capital than any other country, that she could more easily transport her goods from her maritime supremacy, and that there was a world market before her, gradually drew more and more of her population to manufactures—and first to the textile (cotton, woollen, linen, worsted, lace, silk) industries. She could easily sell cheaper than her competitors, though at highly profitable rates ; and, when she had complete monopoly, at still higher rates. She attained the like supremacy in the hardware trades, as well as in the production of iron and steel through the inventions of Bessemer and others. She attained commercial supremacy, and enjoyed it for more than half a century. It was about 1838 that Cobden began the Free Trade crusade in England which was successful in 1846. He preached universal free trade, but he was thinking mainly of the advantage to manufacturers like himself of the removal of all duties on corn, food in general, and the raw materials of manufacture, especially of cotton, altogether drawn from America in his time. Cheap food and raw materials would mean low cost of production, because wages might be reduced; and then with the start we had we could easily maintain our hold on the cotton and other similar industries, if only foreigners would so far imitate us as not to lay on protective duties. He was mistaken in supposing that cheap food for labourers would mean lower wages, for in fact they rose from Trade Union pressure, and still higher from the demand (still rising after 1846) for their labour; but the foreigners would not take off their duties on our manufactures. Had they indeed all done so, England, if she could only have produced enough, would have conquered in each of their markets and destroyed the industries by selling cheaper. She would then have recovered her old monopoly of the first fifty years of the nineteenth century. But it is clear that England could not have made soft goods for all the world without receiving high prices—scarcity prices, in fact—a worse thing for the purchaser than monopoly prices, which are not necessarily high. Still less could she have made iron and steel for all the world without high prices. And so of the rest. If indeed she could have got her population to increase fast enough, she might have produced enough without high prices. But this she could not do, and Mill, the theorist of free trade, as Cobden was the popular preacher, advised the labourers to aim at lessened population. So that the full triumph of free trade would have been high prices and great profits for English manufacturers, ironmasters, and coalmasters (coal being so much in demand), and good wages for the working classes; prices higher abroad than those at which they could produce for themselves, and, be it noted, equally high prices at home for all consumers owing to the limited supply, our country being unequal to the demand of the world. For Cobden's own particular trade it would literally have been a case of Lancashire making cottons for the world and fabulous fortunes for the manufacturers.

The foreigners did not adopt free trade.

They started the textile industries, and they found it necessary to put on duties. They were 'suitable' industries. They came within the scope of Mill's exception to free trade, which he allows in the case of a young country or colony suitable for the creation of a special industry. And why not the restoration of a suitable one in an old country, as well as the creation of it in a new one?

Thus, then, free trade, even one-sided, admirably suited England in 1846, while free trade and free imports still suit her best on the whole, though if we are to think rather of a self-sufficient Empire than of the United Kingdom, it would not suit such an Empire. But continuing to look at the question from the United Kingdom rather than the Empire point of view, we find now, sixty years after Cobden's victory, that while we have no longer a monopoly of certain industries, we have still the lead so far that other countries still find it necessary, or their industrial leaders say it is necessary, to maintain their high tariffs against us. And this they do, sometimes raising, sometimes reducing them, but on the whole raising them and depriving us of more and more of a share in their market. Germany, France, America, Belgium all do so. Russia and Italy are following their example.

Even our colonies, Australia and Canada, who have started manufactures, do the same, more or less, and shut us out. It therefore becomes an urgent matter with us, since having largely transformed ourselves into a nation producing for the foreign market, we require a constant sale for our goods, and even an increasing sale in order to meet the normal increase of population. But the fact is that our exports have been almost stationary for some years. We are not, indeed, threatened with ruin, and the alarm raised is unnecessary. Still it behoves us to look to the future to see what mitigations or improvements are possible. Can our government, following the example of other countries, do anything to benefit our industries? Or must we leave the matter to the energy and intelligence of our captains of industry, promoters, and financiers, who have more than once saved the situation and maintained the lead for England?

As to the first question, it divides itself into two. Could our statesmen do aught for industry by adopting a policy of retaliation, in reply to a rise in the foreign duties? Secondly, could we come to some arrangement other than retaliation in the case of our colonies, some friendly arrangement under which they would agree to lower their tariffs in our favour in return for a *quid pro quo* ;

or, if this is not possible, some agreement that they will not raise them unnecessarily, and that they will give us a preference in all cases over our rivals ?

Those are the two means proposed to restore our export market. Let us consider each in their order, under the light which the short history just given has afforded. But as a necessary preliminary let us first briefly consider the most salient facts and figures respecting our Imports and Exports, together with the conclusions to which they point.

CHAPTER II

PRESENT FACTS AND FIGURES, AND WHAT THEY IMPLY

THE advantages of foreign trade to a country, however inadequately conceived by many, are sufficiently clear and indisputable. The consumers of a country like England get commodities not otherwise accessible at all, such as tea, coffee, rice, wine, spices, diamonds, gold, silver, the rarer sorts of foreign manufacture; and they get things that could have been produced at home but with greater labour, and in consequence at higher prices, such as corn, meat, tobacco, dairy produce, hides. To these may be added the materials of some of our most important manufactures, such as raw cotton, silk, wool, and flax (in part); also the materials of many other industries, such as timber and iron (in part), together with many things in a partially manufactured state which have to undergo further processes before reaching the consumer.

The consumer, according to Mill, is the sole person benefited by foreign trade, and the benefit consists either in getting new desirable things or luxuries, or else old desirable things, whether necessaries or luxuries, on easier terms. The gain does not come, as vulgarly conceived, from the great profits of producers and merchants, exporting or importing; for if foreign trade were abolished altogether, manufacturers who make for profit would turn their capital to the production of the nearest substitutes for the imported commodities, on which they would receive as high profits as before. Importing and exporting merchants would indeed be gone, but they or others would turn themselves into dealers and distributors of the substituted goods and receive their usual gains, while presumably as many labourers would be employed in the making of the substitutes.

But in this view of the matter Mill overlooks, or does not sufficiently emphasise, certain aspects of the facts. He overlooks the fact that if foreign trade were abolished, and with it cheap food, the law of diminishing returns from land would soon come into disastrous operation, and that the population of the United Kingdom, instead of being 42½ millions, would have probably not amounted to more than half that number;

while the price of wheat, instead of being 28s. a quarter, would very likely have been at least thrice as much. He forgets, too, that the supposed substitutes would have been impossible in many cases, so that neither could the profits be made nor the labourers employed in making them. Moreover, the profits made abroad in Mill's time, and before it, by manufacturers and merchants, were far above the normal and necessary profits supposed to exist within a country, as they were largely the nature of monopoly profits until foreign countries started manufactures on their own account.

It is foreign trade alone that has enabled us to double our population since Mill wrote his 'Political Economy' in 1848, and it has more than doubled the producers and merchants in that trade, and in many industries; it has virtually increased the wages of all labourers by furnishing them with cheap and abundant food, in addition to giving a vast number of them good wages and employment in making the exported goods.

The value of the imports is vast beyond example, amounting in 1902 to some 528 millions sterling. That it is so vast is matter for congratulation. That so great a quantity of it is for consumption, is a sign of our wealth. The whole amount is not, however, consumed in the United

Kingdom, for some 65 millions' worth is re-exported, and sold at a profit in the ports of the Continent, while at least 150 millions represent raw materials which, after being manufactured, are largely exported to all parts of the world.

A large part of the total imports represents the freights due to our shipowners for the carriage of foreign goods to one port of destination, and then another cargo to another, as happily we have nearly a monopoly of the carrying trade. Some 90 millions is set down to this account in the estimate made by the Board of Trade. But this large amount does not represent pure profits, for the shipowner must pay out of it the salaries of the captain and officers of his ships, as well as the wages of the seamen; so far, however, as the latter are British, they get their wages out of it, and the shipowner the profits on his capital except the freight which he receives, not from foreigners, but from home producers, for carrying out British exports, which part is not, of course, paid for by any imports.

Then there is another 80 or 90 millions' worth of the imports that is interest, the return for capital lent by the British investors for foreign or colonial enterprise, or the securities of foreign governments, a splendid annual revenue nearly equal in amount to the rent-roll of the British landlords,

and more than the total value of our imports
and exports in 1800; and this amount is pay-
able to individual investors, not in kind, but
in cash, or Bank of England notes if desired.
That this amount is so large is good for the community at home, though the capital of which it is
the interest does still more good to our colonies
and foreign nations whose wealth and industrial
capabilities it is being employed in developing.
It is a mistake to suppose that the capital so
invested abroad has diminished the employment
of English labour, as its export prevented the
fall of profits in England which would otherwise
have occurred in the absence of new and profitable fields of investment at home, or, as Mill
says, prevented commercial crises which would
otherwise have destroyed it. The export of
capital did not diminish but partly increased the
employment of labour at home so as to supply
the new foreign and colonial market, and it would
have increased it very much more and at better
wages (if the labourers had existed), but for the
fact that some of the capital was employed to
raise up manufactures in competition with those
in England.   And this occurred not merely in the
United States, Russia, and Germany, but in our
own colonies, Canada and Australia.

Thus far as to the gain from the imports.

That their value is so much greater than the exports is no cause for grief, if, as is the fact, the difference is largely payment for services rendered or capital lent.

Let us now turn to the exports, the importance of which is shown by the fact that they are the means of procuring the greater part of the imports, and secondly, that they are the conditions of giving employment and wages to a vast multitude of the population in the cotton, woollen, linen, iron and steel trades, in the hardware, lace, etc., and the various industries subsidiary to them; and any shrinkage in the foreign demand for these goods means privation or loss of employment, while a serious elevation of foreign tariffs in two or three leading countries might mean ruin and starvation to multitudes.

It would not mean absolute national ruin if we were completely shut out from the foreign market. We should still, having the ships, retain a large part of the carrying trade; we should still receive the annual tribute as interest on our capital lent to foreign countries. Our merchants might still, like those of Venice formerly, buy foreign goods and re-sell them at a profit abroad even if foreigners would not purchase our manufactures. And the home market would exist and would give employment to a considerable part of our manu-

facturing population.   But as in some of our staple
manufactures (*e.g.* the cotton) we make three times
the quantity for foreign as compared with home
consumption, a like proportion of the workers
would be thrown out of employment in these
trades.   After a time they or their growing children might be drafted off to produce the nearest
substitutes for the imports formerly received—very
imperfect at best, and impossible in many cases.
Some of the dismissed labourers might find a sub-
sistence on the land now used for pasture.   But
they would be obliged to have recourse to the
Government for protection and new corn laws to
save them from semi-starvation on the land; and,
with protection, after a time part of the new generation might make a scanty living on the land as
they now do in Germany.   In the interim there
would be enormous loss of capital, of acquired
skill; privation and slow starvation, emigration,
and probably social upheavals.   The increase of
population would be necessarily checked, as the
evil days foretold by Mill and Malthus would be
at hand.

With a considerable narrowing of our foreign
market we should have these sad phenomena
only in a much less degree, and that is the
worst that we have to apprehend if our exports
decline.   What we require, in fact, is not merely

no contraction, but a continual expansion in our exports, that our population may continue to increase without their condition deteriorating; even if we are to maintain our existing numbers in the degree of comfort they now happily enjoy (the greater number, at least), it is necessary there be no falling off; while the actual situation in 1902, as revealed by official figures, as regards our exports is that they are barely increasing, and have not greatly increased for twenty years. The falling off in some exports has, indeed, been made up for during the past few years by the export of ships and coal—that is, in the latter case, by a part of the efficient force of all our manufactures, which is itself of limited amount.

Let us turn now to only three possible means of enlarging our export markets, namely, retaliation or negotiation, preferential tariffs, and successful competition in the neutral market.

CHAPTER III

RETALIATION

In considering the question of retaliation, it must be first allowed that every independent State has full right to impose whatever duties it pleases on commodities imported from other countries. It has the right to decide the forms in which foreign nations shall have the benefit of selling in its markets. It may let them in duty free; it may raise duties to the point which excludes them altogether. The government of the State in commercial matters is under no obligation to consult any other interest than the weal of that State on the whole.

But, fortunately, the governments of our chief competing nations do not in general consider it good policy to exclude altogether the goods of other countries, and in particular those of England; partly because the consumers in a country wish them to be admitted on account of their lower price or better quality, partly because enlightened

statesmen think the exclusion of all outside competition tends to the arrest of industrial progress.
They prefer to put on such duties as will still
allow some outside competition and give a choice
to the consumer while adequately protecting the
home producer.

The amount of the duty that would allow,
let us say, England to compete on fair terms in
the German market would correspond to the
difference in the costs of production; or, to be
more explicit, the wholesale prices in the two
countries. Thus, suppose cloth of the same kind
and quality were selling at 4s. a yard in Germany
and 3s. a yard in England, a duty of 1s. a yard
(33⅓ per cent.) on imported English cloth would
nearly equalise the positions of the competitors,
and would give the German consumer a choice
of goods. But the greater supply thence result-
ing would tend to reduce the price somewhat
below 4s., and this would injure the German
manufacturer, and also be lower than the average
producer in England could sell at. The price
of 4s. could hardly be maintained, and only the
greater and more successful firms could afford to
accept of less and still make good profits. The
average producers could not, and in Germany
they might complain and get the duty raised to
1s. 3d. a yard instead of 1s. The result would

shut out all English goods except those that had
been making more than ordinary profits, or had
a less cost of production than ordinary, which
would be chiefly the large businesses ably con-
ducted, or those possessed of a patented process
or other superior methods.

Let the duty be raised 10 per cent. higher
and some of these also will have to retire; let
it be raised 10 per cent. more and the German
manufacturers will probably have the trade all to
themselves. They need only then form a big
Trust to have the consumer in Germany completely at their mercy. They might raise their
price to double the English price, and perhaps
higher, by limiting the supply, which could be
most effectively done by sending a part to other
countries, like England, at low prices. Thus
then, the situation would be : double the price to
the German consumer, high profits to the Trust
at home, and a low price abroad—just low
enough to undersell the English producer, who
would suffer doubly: first, by the high excluding
tariff; secondly, by the underselling in England,
which, if continued, might ruin the English producer and drive him from his business.

We have admitted that a statesman is only
bound to consider the good of his own country.
The justification for the duties is that without

them his country will go to the wall, and certainly no country has a right to expect an advantage in the markets of another country at the cost of the industry of that country, if the advantage can be neutralised, as it can be, by means of equalising or higher duties. England has no reasonable ground of complaint at being shut out from the chance of a successful competition which might greatly injure or ruin the German manufacturers ; but she has reason for remonstrance if not only her advantage is neutralised, but she is excluded altogether from the German market. Only strong reasons will justify this. Her Foreign Minister has the right to urge, through the English Ambassador, that, apart from the interests of German consumers, who are injured by the exclusion of cheaper English goods, there is a loss to the English manufacturers ; and that, so long as we admit German manufactures without any duty whatever, even when they have an advantage over ours and can be produced cheaper, it is unequal, if not unfriendly, treatment. The German statesman can reply : ' But you let our manufactures in without duties because you think it best on the whole for yourselves. We do the same in excluding yours. If you put duties on, you will only hurt yourself on your own avowed principles of free trade.'

The only possible reply that can be made is : 'If you shut us out from your markets by exclusive or excessive duties, we may, in spite of our past professions and in our altered circumstances, be compelled, in self-defence, to imitate you. We grant you your right to protect your industries and to save them from being destroyed by foreign competition, but as the argument is the very same, and applies equally to the case of England, we claim the same right for ourselves— namely, to put on an equalising tax, or even an exclusive one, where our manufactures are in danger from your competition.'

It might then be conceded that there was no intention of shutting out English goods altogether, but only competing ones in certain special cases and for certain special reasons, while laying on only an equalising duty as the general rule. But when reasons are offered a door is opened for counter-reasons, and thus for negotiation generally before going the length of retaliation.

We abandoned protection after 1846 because we had no need of it in manufactures owing to our superiority in nearly every branch, and because in agriculture, where we did adopt protection, the free traders proved to be the

stronger party ; and the result has been to place
us in great difficulty as regards effective retaliation, as the only way in which it could be done
hitherto was by placing an additional revenue
duty on imported commodities that we did not produce, such as wines or spirits, while leaving food
and the raw materials of our manufactures untaxed.
At present there is a wider range of taxable commodities from Germany and the United States—
chemical products, oil, machines, manufactured
goods that we do not produce, together with
some that we do, such as glass, silk, iron and
steel, paper, leather, cotton and linen yarns, etc., of
which we imported in 1902 from Germany to the
amount of over 16 millions sterling, and more
from America, part however being only semi-
manufactured. In the case of fully-manufactured
goods we have the means of retaliating if the
German minister of finance or commerce un-
duly or unreasonably raises the German tariff on
us. No doubt each negotiator is inclined to take
a somewhat partial view of the case of his own
country. But, also, statesmen and diplomatists
are usually above the special prejudices of their
countrymen. They are men of clear intellect
who have an interest in effecting a working solution of difficulties by mutual compromise, so as to
avoid the *ultima ratio* which, in the present case,

is not war but retaliation or commercial war, in which, as in other wars, each country inflicts an injury on the other as well as on itself (or rather on the consumers in the other country), but with a final view of peace and a Treaty of Commerce, which might just as well have been made without the tariff war if men were creatures of pure reason. Now the negotiators are usually such beings, more or less, even when they represent nations who are by no means composed of such, and accordingly we might expect that the clumsy weapon of retaliation would seldom be resorted to.

Still, if retaliation became necessary, it would perhaps be better in the first instance to put a duty on products non-competing with ours, such as wines; but if these were not sufficiently important in their aggregate value, and if food and raw materials must be exempted, then it might be necessary to have recourse to manufactures in competition with our own. In this case the duty, though intended merely to be retaliatory, would be in effect protective, though not put on for purposes of protection. Though I should say that, if in addition to being retaliatory they also protected an important industry threatened with destruction, it would be no argument against it save to the extreme and uncompromising free trader.

There could only be at first a rather rough rule or principle of equity to guide our negotiators, but it would become more exact by application to special cases. Thus: we will let your manufactures in duty free, wherever your price for the same class of goods is equal to ours; and again, whenever the commodity is not produced by us at all, provided you will do the same in each case. Where costs of production, or rather prices, are unequal in the two countries, we allow you the right to put on a duty equal to the difference (the only natural duty) if we have the advantage; also to put it higher if you choose. In either case, especially the latter, we reserve the right to do the same, but whether we avail ourselves of it or not will depend on our sense of equity, a general calculation of the balance of advantages, and the special circumstances of the case.

It may be well, however, to indicate more specifically the commoner classes of cases that would arise, which are such as the following :—

(1) When a British industry in some of its specialties is so strong as to be able to compete in the foreign market notwithstanding adverse duties, and where at the same time Germany

has such an advantage in another variety or branch of the same industry—*e.g.* the cotton—and places a duty on the English one higher than corresponds to the 'difference in prices,' we would be justified in doing the like—that is, in placing a duty on the German imports into England. Equity, indeed, would justify us in going farther. If our superiority is so great that the Germans do not compete, but have left this branch of the production to us, in that case we would be justified in retaliating if Germany put any duty on this class of goods. It would only be a revenue duty in Germany, since by hypothesis there is nothing to protect where the industry has been left to us.

(2) If Germany is so efficient that she can compete with us on equal terms in our market, this is a case of equality, and in this case, as before said, Germany ought to remove her duty, or we should put on an equal amount in our market. Reciprocity, equality of treatment, might claim more. If Germany is better than we in a certain class of goods, a duty equal to the difference might be put on if Germany did the like where we are stronger.

But in both cases it would be better to take off duties in regard to specialties or varieties in which each excels; and instead of

retaliation, or a mutual raising for the sake of
equality, a mutual lowering in this case would be
better. That is, retaliation is to be used as a
means of securing equity, which a lowering of the
duty on the part of Germany would equally secure.

Retaliation may be used unless Germany
reduces her adverse duty in a similar case. For
example, if it would be necessary for us, in order
to compete, to put on an equalising duty of 20
per cent., let Germany reduce by 20 per cent. in
a corresponding case, or we put on the duty.
The situation is, 'We will not put on, if you will
take off an equal percentage in an analogous and
specifically named case, or some other case held
by us to be of equal importance, and not merely
in the case of an insignificant industry.'

This applies to the manufactures imported
from all countries. But we could not apply it
to America to induce her to lower her tariffs,
except as regards the comparatively small amount
of manufactures obtained from her, such as iron,
implements, boots, paper, oil, the total value
of which is not great, only some 10 millions
sterling. It could not, of course, be applied to
food or raw materials or partly worked-up
materials.

(3) In a case where we have let in the German
productions free and they have gradually gained

on us, and finally are pressing us close, whether by patented methods, better organisation, technical skill and knowledge, or even lower wages, we should not protect, especially if we started on equal terms and Germany gained on us by fair competition.   But there are exceptions which in the last necessity would justify protection.   If one of our great staple industries, involving various subsidiary industries and the employment of hundreds of thousands of hands was being beaten, we should be justified in protecting the industry.   Happily the case is not likely to arise. But of course in such a case, long before Germany got ahead of us she should have been requested to cease the protection in Germany which was no longer needed.   As soon as it was perceived that she was gaining in our market and able to undersell us, not merely in varieties, but generally, our statesmen should have required Germany to lower her tariffs in proportion to her growing superiority ; and if she had refused, we should have put on duties as retaliatory duties much sooner.   She would hardly refuse in this case, but it would only benefit those who had the lowest cost of production in England.

(4) In a case where Germany was superior from the first, having created the industry, we should not give protection to producers in Eng-

land to enable them to start a competing industry. But in a like case where we instituted an
industry, Germany should not try to spoil our
game and share the gains by rearing a similar
one under protection; or, if she did, we should
not indeed imitate her by starting a competing
industry under protection, but hit a different
industry of hers, whether in competition with us
or not.

(5) Where both nations are doing fairly well,
having started equal, as in the chemical and the
iron and steel trade, the aim should be for each
to let in the varieties and specialties of the other
at as low rates as possible. There is no reason
whatever for protection in Germany, and if she
protects against us, common fairness and self-
defence requires us to do the like; and in such
a clear case a statesman who recognises that
there is such a thing as international equity
would at once see that the duties should be taken
off, otherwise our statesmen would fail in their
duty to their country's interest if they did not
threaten a course of reprisals which would probably bring the other side to reason and justice.
In the case under consideration *low* duties or *no*
duties are the thing to be aimed at, but if any, the
same on both sides.

In the first case, in the end the industry will

be divided between the two countries, and little competition will exist as to those branches in which each is superior, while it may continue for a long time in respect to the more ordinary qualities of the commodity; and in this case, as already stated, if we let in German goods free, she should do the same, there being no need of protection on either side. Fortunately, the tendency is in this direction. Germany sends us certain kinds of linen or woollen, or certain classes of yarns in which she excels. We do the like. *She* puts on duties; we do not. But if we let in her best goods duty free and retire from the competition, she should lower her duties on our best which she does not produce in the same industry. Now a good deal of trade does subsist between the countries, even in the products of industries that each is engaged in. This part of the trade might be entirely free, and we should then have a real example of the benefits of foreign trade, because each would be producing both for itself and the other nation that which it could produce best and cheapest.

The commercial policy of all statesmen should aim so far at free trade. Wherever a nation has such a decided lead—either in a whole industry (though this will be rare) or in any of the different classes of goods or varieties into which it usually splits up—as to have no competitors left, it is best to remove the duties. It is no case for protection where the other nations, for some reasons, have retired from or not entered the competitive field, and it is hardly a good case for revenue duty, except so far as it is likely to produce a good yield to the Customs. But if one nation makes it its policy to tax at the entrance, others may have to do the same, though it is not protective.

The above are specimens of the kinds of cases that may arise, and of the equitable considerations that apply to them; cases that could easily be multiplied and which will become more specialised if we adopt a policy of reciprocity. I think it well to give some examples in order to show the reader that we have a real case for negotiation, and that we might benefit ourselves in important cases by the policy, without much hurt to the other side.

As for the assertion that retaliation always results in increasing the evil, as in the tariff wars between France and Italy, and between Germany and Russia, I think that it need not be so. There is no good reason why it should be so. Statesmen having the care of great interests must not be supposed to act on principles hurtful to those interests. They must be supposed to do what they think is for the good of their respective nations; and able and honest ones, in estimating that good, take account of the different powerful, and sometimes clashing, interests within the nation. For instance, in Germany there is the divergent interest of the Agrarian party and all the consumers of manufactures on one side, and that of the German manufacturer on the other. The consumers are composed of the Agrarians and all persons outside the manufacturing interest, and all of these are opposed to high tariffs on our goods, which mean high prices to them. Nay, the consumer is often a producer concerned with one branch of manufacture, and would be glad to see the tariff removed from all but his special branch—whether woollen, or linen, or iron—and he only defends it in other cases because he thinks his own case is involved with them. The taking off a tariff would directly benefit everybody except those connected with that one industry. It does not therefore follow if our Minister (of Commerce, suppose) complained of an increase of, say, 15 per cent. *ad valorem* on linen exports to Germany and succeeded in preventing it, that anyone would grieve in Germany except those connected with the linen interest; or if any other did, it would be on the principle that 'our turn may come next,' which might produce a certain solidarity amongst manufacturers in general. But even so, the agrarian interest is so powerful in the Reichstag and the country that it might favour the reduction of the duty, and such is alleged to be the existing feeling in Germany; so that we should have powerful allies there if our minister threatened retaliation in the case of a proposed rise of duties. In most cases we should have the consumers on our side, and what alone saves the producers and gets them protection is the statesman's belief that the producers of a country, in spite of the consumers—who, in the long run, depend on them—must be protected from destructive foreign competition.

With respect to the all too celebrated 'dumping' cases, such as those of manufactured goods sold cheaply in England while the same class of goods of ours are shut out from the United States and Germany by high tariffs, that is a thing which ought not to be allowed to continue, as it sins doubly against fairness; and even those who practise it in America are somewhat shy to speak of it or defend it. They first put their tariff so high that we cannot get in at all, or barely, because it would take away all profit, being greater than the difference between English and American prices; then these same manufacturers who enjoy this protection against our competition

E

send their surplus productions to our market and
undersell us ; and it pays them to do so because,
if they forced a sale at home in case of too great
a supply, their prices would necessarily come
down so much that they would get less for the
whole supply than they do for a part at the
higher prices.   It is merely an ingenious way of
limiting supply and getting the benefits of such a
questionable practice, because it keeps all the
hands at work, and only inflicts evil on their
own consumers and our manufacturers, whose
industries it might even ruin as well as deprive
workmen of a livelihood, while protected rivals
across the Atlantic or the German Ocean were
pocketing high profits at the expense of their
own countrymen.

Our manufacturers here suffer doubly : first, in
being excluded from all access to the American
market (the Americans being the worst offen-
ders in this line, and the inventors of the practice), where they could undersell the Americans ;
secondly and much worse, in being attacked
by those who cannot meet us in open and fair
competition, with essentially unfair and almost
immoral competition.   This too smart American
practice of hitting their own countrymen by high
prices and then (as a salve) hitting their rivals
by low prices in England, must be prevented,

because it is questionable international morality to be excluded from the American markets by high tariffs, and then to be pursued into our own and perhaps ruined if the practice be sufficiently long continued. It is a practice which urgently demands government interference, and it requires to be stopped in the interest of the American consumer as well as of our producers; for though it is no part of an English minister's business to undertake a crusade for the consumer abroad, yet when the abatement of a nuisance and an evil to ourselves benefits him, the matter can be comparatively easily settled, as we should have his hearty support in our negotiations. A sufficiently high duty put on by us, or such as would equalise the American with the English price, would stop the evil for one consequence; and for a second it would cause the prices to fall in America, so that if limitation of supply be necessary or desirable, the trust would have to try another course.

Our manufacturers of themselves are perfectly powerless in this kind of competition. They cannot hit back their rivals serenely sheltered in America behind the tariff walls. As things are they cannot protect themselves, and if the invasion by the trust-produced goods was sufficiently long continued and sufficiently large, our manufacturers would infallibly be ruined and driven out of the business. 'All the better,' says some un-shrinking free traders. 'Let them dump away. They are giving us goods at half-price. Who would refuse a present?' But, suppose they succeed in driving the English producer out as they did their rivals in America—what do you suppose they will then do? They will strengthen their combination in America, get more capital if necessary, and produce just enough and no more than enough to supply the British market, no longer at the cheap dumping-prices, but precisely as high as they think compatible with their own interest. They will limit supply or not, with the same end. But the strong probability is that the prices would be the American prices, which were 50 per cent. over the English ones, and so instead of the English pulling down the American prices, which without the tariff they would have done, the prices in England will be raised to the American level, our English industries will be ruined, and the workmen will be either pauperised or forced to emigrate to America to do the work there instead of in England.

CHAPTER IV

PREFERENTIAL TARIFFS

I

THE second plan for widening our market for exports aims at securing as much as possible of the colonial market for our manufactures, by a system of mutual preferences. The colonies give us a preference of 33⅓ per cent. less duty than is levied on the goods of any other nation, and we in return are to give them an advantage by placing a duty on corn or other foodstuffs imported from all nations excepting the colonies. At present the colonies give us a preference over our competitors without asking anything in return, partly on grounds of sentiment, but also, as a Canadian statesman said, because it was for their own interest in Canada. In no case does it involve much sacrifice, as the British manufacturers without the preference can beat their competitors ; so that giving it does not tend, as preferences generally do, to raise prices to the Canadian consumer, but the reverse. What does raise the price is the tax they still impose even on the most favoured nation's goods. Not the less is the preference of considerable value to us. It ensures that whatever is bought will be bought from us, and that is something considerable as proved by the value of the exports of manufactures to all the self-governing colonies for last year, which amounted to 52 millions sterling.

But so far there is not much reason why we should give anything in return for a favour that costs the Canadians nothing but a slight reduction of their Customs revenue, though we might be willing to give something for it if it was threatened to be taken away; but not much, as it has not greatly increased our trade with Canada.

For the fact remains that Canada places heavy protective duties on some of our manufactured goods, with a view to protect her own manufactures in competition with ours (such as the cotton and iron industries), and also duties on non-competing manufactures ; the duties in the latter case being for revenue, in the former for protective purposes. In the latter case, we supply the whole market, though under high duties ; in the former, the duties are so high as to be almost exclusive, and we should do little trade but for the fact that the manufactures in the colonies are in a comparatively undeveloped state, and cannot supply the choicer and finer classes of goods which, if the richer people will have them, they must take from us. Now it is only with respect to these two latter kinds of manufacture that there is any room for anything in the nature of a bargain or commercial treaty between us and the colonies.

They have established certain manufactures by the aid of protective duties, as they had a full right to do by the constitutions granted to them by the Imperial Government, and they cannot adopt free trade without injuring vested interests and important classes, though by so doing they would benefit the colonial consumers. All that the colonial governments can do to further reduce their markets for us is to lower their tariffs for revenue, and perhaps their protective tariffs so far as to allow us to compete on equal terms ; and for this, added to the preference already given, we should be ready to give something in return. A preferential duty on corn would be the best *quid pro quo*. It would give an impetus to the production of wheat in Canada and Australia, especially in the former, of great importance to us in the near future in view of the rapidly increasing population of the United States, and the consequent great demand of that population added to our own on her corn production, which must, within a moderate period, lead to greatly increased prices, partly from exhaustion of the good soils and resort to inferior ones, partly from increased demand.

It is this fact, and not the fact that we should have within the Empire potential granaries in time of war, that is of significance, for in case of war, unless one with the United States, it is on the latter we must continue to rely. In time of war with any other country, the United States flag would protect our supply of food, which the Americans contend should not be contraband of war. That we had the corn within the Empire would be a most illusory consolation, since it would still have to cross the ocean to England, and would be liable to seizure in British or Colonial ships, while in the ships of the United States it would probably be safe in all cases, unless on the unlikely supposition that we were at war with the United States herself.

It is for the sake of the future that the cultivation of corn, and the agricultural development of Canada generally, is desirable to the people of the British Islands. But the duty on corn would raise the price of the bread of the people it is urged. Well, a 2s. duty would tend to raise it a little—a very little indeed ; but it would also benefit the people now living, or their children hereafter. So far as our market for manufactures expanded in Canada, it would raise wages or prevent them from falling, or labourers from being thrown out of work, as they are being at present in the cotton manufacture in Lancashire. But the chief advantage would come from the development of the corn-growing colonies of Canada (and parts of Australia), especially the former, as being so much nearer to England, and having greater industrial promises. This development would allow population to expand in England, and would attract any surplus population in England to Canada especially, as the real New England and 'land of promise.' It would provide an attractive field for emigrants from these countries, and a vigorous agricultural population would be assured, of great importance in future to Great Britain—both for the purposes of peace and war, in view of the fact that England has largely lost her own agricultural population.

At the present rate of increase the population of Canada will within forty years amount to some 20 millions, able to supply all our necessary corn and in time of war a quarter of a million soldiers. England could supply the manufactures that the increasing population would require, if only the Canadians would let us, and this would provide additional employment in England ; and thus the free trade ideal would tend to be so far realised, because unless higher duties were laid on for the express purpose of shutting out English manufacturers they would have a necessarily increasing market.

The whole object of the policy is to secure wider markets to make up for the loss of part of our markets in countries such as Germany and the United States, which now produce for themselves what they formerly bought from us. At present Canada gives us a preference of 33⅓ per cent. We are the 'most favoured nation,' but Canada still keeps the duties very high against us. We do a fair trade with her and it is greater since we got the preference, but still the question is, Can the colonial governments not do still more in our favour without hurt to their own interests if we give a preference to some of their exports and especially corn? Can Canada lower her still high tariffs on those of our manufactures which do not compete with hers and, still more important, can she lower her protective tariff and engage not to protect new industries such as flourish in the United Kingdom, unless Canada is specially suited for such or unless they were such as it would be desirable for her to create if she were completely independent of Great Britain?

If so much cannot be guaranteed—and it is

doubtful if it can be, or if future statesmen would hold themselves bound by such concession—there is no place for friendly bargaining and matters must remain as they are.   And certainly on our side statesmen will not be able to place duties on corn, still less corn and meat, in favour of Canada without a lowered tariff, nor would even that be sufficient reason for departure from our settled free trade policy under which we have on the whole greatly prospered, unless there were other prospective advantages, both economic and political, to be gained by the change.

We may go so far as a 2s. preference, which will benefit Canadian farmers and not do us much harm, nor the Americans in the long run, as it will prevent the ultimate rise in price in the United States from increased demand and greater expense of production.   We might even go so high as 4s.; but we could not do more without hurting our people at home, unless the Canadians can reduce their tariffs ; and we cannot benefit them further by giving them preference on meat and dairy produce without raising prices for their benefit, and not for the benefit of our farmers in the United Kingdom, who have been specially injured by the free imports of foreign cattle and meat and dairy produce, as their fathers were by the free import of corn.

II

It is quite true there are political as well as economic considerations involved in the question. Canada is a growing country with a great future ; all the facts point that way—her newly discovered goldfields, her boundless and fruitful fields for the finest wheat, her marvellously increasing imports and exports, her rapid general development, her fast increasing population recruited by the immigration of over 100,000 yearly, in addition to the normal increase of a vigorous colony. She has 6½ millions now ; she will have, at the past rate of increase of the United States, within fifty years 25 millions of people, and there is no reason to think the rate will be less.

She will then have the population of a great State, nearly as much as the present population of Italy, more than that of Spain, and it is a natural and interesting question, Will she go the way of her great sister State across her southern border and become independent, in accordance with the general law that an organism already largely leading an independent life, as it becomes fully able to sustain and defend itself naturally seeks the ampler freedom of action and of development which complete independence alone

allows, and which every connection and every
form of federation in some degree hinders?

Will she form a union with the great people
of common blood and common language with
whom she has material and economic ties, from
which she is separated merely by an invisible
boundary line for thousands of miles of frontier,
or, rather, will the present connection continue
with England, the mighty Empire that has nurtured her and defended her in two wars with the
United States, and with whose forces her sons
have bravely fought in those same wars as well
as in our recent South African war?

The fact is Canada is now somewhat in the
interesting situation of a rich heiress with two
suitors—two rich and prosperous cousins—John
Bull and Brother Jonathan. Material considerations would rather seem to favour a union with the
latter, which Goldwin Smith thinks her 'manifest
destiny.' But she herself has a strong sentimental
leaning to the former, derived from history, the
strongest of all kinds of ties. She admires John
for his feudal lineage, his aristocratic air, his
European culture, rather than her somewhat
ordinary cousin across the border who, though
equally rich, appears in her eyes to be somewhat
of the parvenu. Then she has had quarrels with
the latter and she is not easily reconciled.

In plainer language, there is in favour of a closer and a permanent union with Great Britain the existing connection as a fact, and the expressed desire of Canadian statesmen for a closer union. She has no desire to become a state or a cluster of states added to the United States. That is not her ideal, whatever else is. A large part of the Canadians have no friendly feeling for the United States, arising from the fact that their ancestors (their grandfathers and great-grandfathers) fought against them and for England in two bloody wars ; and it seems that they have longer memories and cherish enmity longer than the generous-hearted people across the frontier, who readily forget and forgive and admire the sons or grandsons of former enemies. The result is that Canada prefers the English connection to the only other even possible one ; so that if the union is not with England, Canada will set up for herself. She will ask for, and she will get, complete independence, like the United States and Mexico, and all the States of South America.

We should all be sorry. We should much prefer her to remain in an even closer union, or at the least as she now is related to us. She has borne the brunt of two invasions in our quarrel, which she made hers ; she has aided us in South Africa, and when she has 20 millions of people her aid might be of great import to us in a possible war. Still, looking at the matter from the 'family solicitor' point of view, it might prove too high a price for the possible advantages of such a union if we had to reverse completely for it our fiscal policy under which we have marvellously prospered, give up our free trade faith and practice and become protectionist to please her, while she remains strictly and rigidly protectionist against us. It is possible to pay too high a price for a self-sustaining Empire, or even Imperial Federation.

It is, however, asserted by Mr. Chamberlain that if we do not do so, and do so soon, we shall lose Canada and lose the colonies generally and so descend to the position of a third-rate power; descend from our pride of place and empire to be a small carrier country like Holland formerly. But is this likely? Is it likely the colonies will drift away from us? Certainly not at present, though it is on the cards that Canada will one day do so, and she is nearer to her majority than Australia.

However, let us face the worst contingency. Let us suppose Canada one day, from substantial and not sentimental grounds, joined the American Union. We should regret it; it would imply a loss of prestige and possible future power to England;

it would mean also some loss of trade, but it would not be the ruin of England. Even in the more likely case of her becoming an independent nation, which she can become if she chooses as soon as ever she can stand alone, though we should greatly regret the loss, it would not by any means, not even if Australia followed her example, reduce us to the position of a third-rate nation. We should still be a great Empire with at least 42 millions of people, and with India, the 'brightest gem in the Imperial Crown,' containing 250 millions more. We should still, in fact, be more populous at home than France or any civilised nation except Russia, Germany, and the United States, with two of which we are not likely ever to be at war, though if unhappily it should ever be otherwise in the case of the latter, the severance of the tie with Canada would be the deliverance from a great danger.

Then it must not be overlooked that if Canada became completely independent, as she is now nearly so, we should still as she develops have trade with her, either with a preference as now proposed, or without it ; since even if she became independent she would still desire a market for her goods, and we form the natural and nearest market for her corn, and indeed for most of her products ; and then she necessarily must always have a peculiar feeling for the mother nation which nurtured her and defended her in the past, and that feeling will force her to give the old country the 'most favoured nation' treatment in commerce, and not improbably in case of a war it might induce her to form an alliance as useful to England as if she were a member of an Imperial federation. The only difference would be that under a federal system she would be bound to contribute her quota, whereas now it is optional, as it would be if she were independent.

III

The case of Australia is markedly contrasted with that of Canada. She is a continent as large as Canada; but she is at the opposite side of the globe. Canada is only six or seven days' voyage distant; Australia four times as much. The climate of Australia is not so good nor the soil in general so fertile, and it is subject to destructive droughts. There are few great navigable rivers; only the fringe of the country appears to have good land for cultivation. Still, it has good corn-growing land, and the vine flourishes. There is gold and coal, and great tracts of pasture which support millions of sheep. The population is small, half of it being concentrated in three large towns—

F

Sydney, Melbourne, and Adelaide, with their suburbs. The rest of the people are farmers, miners, artisans, and shepherds. The country does not increase rapidly in population; at present, strange to say, there is emigration from it to Argentina, which may, however, be only a temporary evil. On the whole it does not appear to have so promising a future before it as Canada.

With regard to the question of preference it does not appear that we can do more with prudence than in the case of Canada—namely, give her exemption from the moderate corn duty of 2s. a quarter, though she has heavier freights to pay, and her crop is less to be relied on, owing to possible drought. We cannot give her wool preferential treatment without handicapping our woollen and worsted industries in their competition with France and Germany. It is sufficient that we give her a free market for her abundant goods and wool. Besides, she does not much fear the competition of other nations in wool. She has also a free market for her frozen meat that she cannot get elsewhere. She has already gained much from the English Imperial connection. Besides a market for her wool and her meat, the latter formerly of little use but now valuable, she got the best investment for her new gold; later on, she got the use of abundant English capital for the development of her resources; this, no doubt, was good for both, though perhaps part of it might have been better invested than in the creation of manufactures by means of protective duties to compete with those of England. The only advantage she offers us as regards the present question is, while raising the duties on foreign manufactures, to let them remain at the existing rather high scale as against ourselves. There is, however, one rather more encouraging fact. New South Wales is for free trade with us, and there our market may increase as well as in other parts where her manufactures are not so fully developed as ours, or where they produce inferior varieties not really in competition with our goods. These, though nominally called the same, are really different classes of goods, the result of inferior methods, machinery, and labour, and are ranked by the purchaser accordingly.

So far as Australian statesmen have influence they should, with respect to projected competing industries, only allow the assistance of the government in the way of protective duties to industries specially suitable to the circumstances of the country. The difficulty is how to prevent English capital from going to Australia to develop new competing industries and to get the expected benefit of the general Australian tariff. Go the capital will from England, whether the industrial chief accompanies it or not; and the most promising industries in the eyes of the capitalist or company promoter it will start, and then the usual protection duty will be asked against foreign competition, and most of all against that of England, as the most dangerous. The statesman and the legislature in most cases must lay on the duty, as the Australian interests come before Imperial interests. So that colonial Premiers can in no case say, with respect to a proposed industry, 'Why not leave this industry to Great Britain? She can supply the commodity far better and cheaper.' Astute men, promoters and financiers, probably in England even, ask themselves, 'Where is there a good opening?' They meditate, and such and such an industry occurs to their fertile brain. The promoter thinks he is sure of the tariff on his side, and starts the concern. He cannot be prevented. To the legislature it would seem invidious and unpatriotic not to support an enterprise which promised to give employment to home labour, and so the thing is launched.

The Australian statesman does not desire the powers of the legislature in this respect to be narrowed, nor to hinder home enterprise. The

English statesman is still more powerless, the Imperial Parliament having deliberately and solemnly given a free hand to the colony in respect of fiscal matters.

The conclusion is that, having given Australia the same advantage as respects corn as Canada, we should go no further unless she can lower her tariffs, which probably she cannot. If she could, the duty might be raised on such wines as compete with Australian wine; but only these and by a small percentage of their value. It would help the wine trade in Australia, and would do little harm to anyone in the United Kingdom except middle-class drinkers of moderate-priced claret or burgundy or hock.

Otherwise leave things to their natural course. Australia likes the connection, from which, up to the present, she has profited far more than Canada, and which is still very beneficial to her; in fact, far more than to us. She knows very well 'on which side her bread is buttered,' as the phrase goes. We are bound to protect her in case of war without any expense on her part; but as any war is likely to be much more England's concern, it seems fair that she should only contribute as much as she might reasonably be supposed by her own statesmen to expend on her own defence if she were

independent.   That amount she is spared, and
then she is not asked either for a contribution
for Imperial defence nor a quota for the Army
—in a word, Australia has altogether the best
of the bargain; some concession is rather due
from her to England, and it is for Australian
statesmen in ordinary gratitude to consider what
form it should most appropriately take.

We owe nothing to South Africa for her preference.   We have spent on behalf of her, as well
as the Empire, 225 millions of money, besides
thousands of precious lives.   She has no manufactures, and our market there is good in consequence, and likely so to continue, since the
legislature in Cape Colony has recommended a
preference of 25 per cent. on English goods.

IV

The conclusion to which we are led is that
free trade should be the rule with England,
mainly because it secures us cheap food and raw
materials, and generally cheap goods; but that
consistently with this aim and with free trade
there may be the following exceptions: (1) A
small and temporary duty on corn from which the
colonies are exempted for reasons both economic
and political, as affording cheap food and a good

field for our emigrants in the future, and in the present or near future a wider market for our exports; (2) possible retaliatory duties in the several cases already mentioned, as well as in the case of trust or cartel produced goods sheltered at home from competition which we could easily meet but for the high duties, and sold cheap to us, to the great danger of destroying and dislocating the same manufactures in England. The object in both cases is to remove or mitigate the cause of the evil—namely, the excessive or unfair duties abroad; and it is clearly defensible on free trade principles, which implies *no* duties to aim at lessening duties. It is asserted that the object will not be attained; but this is contrary to reasons already given and cannot be proved by experience in the case of underselling by trusts, which is a wholly new phenomenon.

These apparent departures from free trade can all be defended on the free trade principles; as well as Mill's case of temporary duties for the raising of an industry for which the circumstances of a country are specially suited, but which cannot be nurtured without the duties.

Our statesmen should go no further, and should tax corn only with a view to assuring cheaper corn in the near future. With regard to meat, there should be no tax on foreign meat

exempting the colonies.   They require no preference, as Australian or New Zealand frozen
meat has an advantage already in being allowed
free access to our market at the cost of our
farmers, though to the benefit of the general public
outside.   The same applies to Canadian cattle.
All that can be said in favour of such a preference
is that, on the side of the farmer of the United
Kingdom, it prevents prices falling rather lower,
but it is against the interest of the non-agri-
cultural consumers who are the most numerous
to-day, though a hundred years ago it was the
reverse.   In fact, the question does really arise
whether in the interest of farmers, agricultural
labourers, and those dependent on these, together
with their families in England, Scotland, Wales,
and Ireland, who still amount to some 12 millions,
and more than that of all the colonies put
together, a protective tax should not be put on?
The farmers have been injured by free trade if
the country as a whole has benefited; and
Ireland, almost wholly an agricultural country,
has specially been injured.   'The political argument,' that it is not good for a nation to lose
its agricultural population, comes in to enforce
their claim.   On that ground and on the ground
of compensation due for injury done for the
benefit of the rest of the community, to preserve

the agricultural population and to prevent their interest from further loss, it might be argued that they should get special protection against *both* the colonies and foreign countries, and this not by a protective tax on corn, but on cattle, dead meat, and dairy produce. They have suffered by free import of corn ; if they are also to suffer by the free import, from all the cheapest quarters of the world, of cattle and all other farm produce they must be more and more depressed. The sacrifice in England has been borne by a past generation as regards corn. The present generation are only injured in respect of their cattle-rearing and dairy produce, and their case certainly deserves the statesman's consideration. Ireland has been compensated to some extent, but she still suffers much by foreign competition in the English market. And I think the issue to be raised here is, either *no* taxes on cattle or meat or dairy produce, or taxes to protect the agricultural interest of the United Kingdom which, now that wheat cultivation is so contracted, suffers more from colonial than foreign competition.

But, on the whole, I should approve of free trade here too, in the interest of the greater number, and especially the working classes. There should, of course, be no tax on raw materials or semi-manufactured goods, to be further worked up, such as wool, raw cotton, silk, flax, yarns, iron ore or iron billets, leather, timber, etc., although such taxes might greatly benefit our colonies which produce some of these materials, if they were exempted from them.

A few words may still be profitably spent on the question, now so much discussed, How far protection pure and simple, as distinct from retaliation, may be advisable in the case of manufactures? We have admitted that Germany may put on a tax to equalise the two costs of production, or, in other words, to raise English prices to equality with German prices, so that her industries may not be destroyed by underselling. On the other hand, has not England the same right to put on a tax where Germany is superior and can sell at less price? It must be allowed she has. But up to the present time she has not cared to exercise it, because in most branches of manufacture she had a superiority and there was no need for it. She had it in cotton, woollen, linen, iron and steel, glass and machinery. Now it is different. Germany is superior to us in the making of chemicals, scientific instruments, musical instruments, certain kinds of woollen and cotton and linen goods and machinery, certain kinds of glass and articles made from glass—bottles, lamp-

shades, etc. She met our producers in competition
and slowly drove them from the market. Now
with respect to a proposed protective tax to prevent a trade from being further injured, it should
be first asked how Germany, beginning on something like equal terms, gained gradually her advantage. It may have been the result of less cost
of production—either from lower wages, the work
done being as efficient as in England ; or longer
hours of work ; or from factory legislation being
less ; or from better business organisation and
management ; or the possession of a patent which
the English rival had not ; or, finally, which is an
extension of the first cause, from ' sweated labour.'
As to the first and second—namely, low wages and
long hours—this is not believed to constitute any
disadvantage to the English employers, the result
of the lower hours and higher wages being as
good as that of the longer hours and lower wages
in Germany, so that there would be no ground
for protection on that score ; and if the Germans
had patented processes or inventions or better
business management, it would not be good
policy to neutralise these two advantages by
a protective duty (unless Germany did the like
to us). And the reason is because it is good
to let the German manufacturer have the advantage his patent or business ability confers,

which will ultimately benefit the English consumer ; and because to deprive him of it by a
tax which would eat up his differential gains
would discourage such inventions and encourage
routine and industrial stagnation in England.
The only sufferers will be inefficient employers
and dismissed workmen, who may lose their
profits and wages.   This is a real evil, but the
less of two evils, the alternative that continually
confronts us in economic and social questions.

On the other hand, we expect that Germany
will give us patent rights in Germany and will
not raise her tariffs simply because our manufacturers have a superior process, or because some of
the best firms can produce at less cost than usual.
We allow of a tax equal to the average difference
of the costs of production, but this should not be
raised owing to these special advantages, or for
any but good reasons—which would mean what
an impartial arbitrator thought good reasons.

Again, the German costs of production and
prices may be less not only because wages are
lower in some cases, but also because the German
manufacturer may content himself with less profits
(as they may be raised in America for the contrary
reasons).   In this way the German may gain a
footing and undersell us.   Should our people be
protected against this ?   It is a doubtful case,

and in doubtful cases we should not depart from free trade, our present principle, as the general rule. The same applies to factory legislation as affecting cost of production. We have more regulations than in Germany, but not to any great extent; and such legislation cannot add much to our cost of production as compared with that in Germany.

As to the products of what is called sweated labour, if we agree to shut out undesirable immigrants because they undersell our labourers by being sweated in England, it would be desirable to shut out the product of their labour even when they remain on the Continent. The thing to be said on the other side is that the product provides cheap but inferior clothing and other commodities for the poorer classes in England.

The only final general answer, both in the case of Germany and England, is that if the superiority of the invading nation is so marked as to be likely to greatly cripple or permanently destroy an established and important industry, protection may be used to prevent it, and if the superiority is again permanently increased the tariff may be raised. But it should never be raised beyond the difference likely to be general and permanent between the two costs of production. Now this does not apply to a patented process, which can only be temporary and partial in its effects, nor to superior. business genius, which likewise lessens costs of production, as such is likely to be rare, and it is for the good of both nations not to discourage it.   No duties, therefore, should be put on or raised merely for reasons of such special advantages.

The conclusion therefore to which we have arrived is that an indiscriminate tax of 10 per cent. on the average on manufactures, as Mr. Chamberlain suggests, would be impolitic and injurious.   All the above applies only to manufactures in competition with us and actually existing.   It does not apply to the case of a proposed new manufacture that we never had, although we have already allowed that a protective duty of a temporary kind might enable us to start such an industry.   But why should we do so if Germany has special facilities for this industry, whether in soil, climate, established connection, trained labourers, etc.?   Could not our promoters and financiers look out for a more promising enterprise, and a new one, in which the facilities and advantages would be on our side, and especially the advantage of first occupation of the field?   Or could they not rather put their capital into the old industries where we still have an indisputable advantage—as proved by the foreign

tariffs against us—and, to make this course profitable, endeavour to widen the neutral or colonial
market ?

We should hardly recommend protection for
this purpose, or even to restore an already de-
feated industry, which is not a hopeful enterprise,
but one which becomes daily more difficult, owing
to the very large capital now necessary. We should
only employ it to preserve an existing one under
the conditions above specified, while even here
the superiority of the foreigner may become so
great that it would be unwise to continue its
defence by constantly raising the tariff as the
foreigners become more efficient.

CHAPTER V

NEUTRAL MARKETS

WE now come to a question the importance of which has been much underrated by both sides in the great debate now before the public, the question whether England might not get compensation for the loss of protected markets, either in foreign countries or the colonies, by selling in the neutral market; that is, in those countries that have no manufactures in our sense of the word— countries such as Argentina, Brazil, South America generally, Mexico, Turkey in Europe and Asia, Persia, China, Morocco, and West Africa under the spheres of British influence.   There is much hope in this, and the Board of Trade figures show that our trade in these countries is increasing, while it is decreasing with Germany, France, and the United States.   For this trade we have great advantages.   The first is that our competitors are obliged to protect themselves against us in their own markets, and this should assure us of victory in the neutral markets. Then we have vast capital, able industrial chiefs, skilled and energetic labourers, and as ingenious inventors and discoverers of new processes as our competitors. Our great commercial marine ought to count as an additional advantage, were it not for the fact that it is at the disposal of foreign manufacturers as well as our own on payment of freight.

But, strange to say, our competitors appear to be gaining on us in the neutral markets, though our exports still increase—and this looks a paradox. They have to defend themselves against us at home by tariffs, thereby admitting our superiority ; yet they beat us in some of the neutral markets. What is the explanation ? In part they supply a different and inferior class of goods, yet to the uncritical purchaser it appears just as good and is cheaper ; and it is a common remark that our business men do not consult their taste or vary their production to meet the varying conditions of the case, that our agents are not as good linguists, or as persuasive, or as good advertisers of the British goods. And there is no denying that our competitors have struck out independent lines of production even when in competition with us, and that they supply goods that we do not produce at all, which they persuade their foreign clients to

G

buy; and of course the more they take from our competitors the less means they have to purchase from us.

If we are to continue to hold our own, we shall have to take a leaf from the books of our chief competitors—the Germans and the Americans; we must develop our technical and commercial schools, press the best ability into business careers, encourage scientific research, for deficiency in which we have ceded the chemical industries to the Germans. We must copy something of their methods, as they copied ours. We taught our competitors our industries and processes. We sent them our machinery; we lent them our capital to assist the development of their industries, though not from philanthropy but from business motives.

If indeed they could beat us and sell in the neutral markets equally good commodities and of the same class at lower prices, and if they could do this in respect to our principal staple industries, the day of England's industrial and commercial supremacy would be gone.

But that day is certainly not yet, in spite of the large increase of German and American exports, nor does it seem to be threateningly near. For if our exports have narrowed in the German and American markets, they have widened in the neutral and in the non-protecting markets during the past six years to 62 per cent. as compared with the remainder of our foreign exports. The fact that the foreign nations find it necessary to place such high duties upon our exported manufactures in their own markets is an acknowledgment of our superiority, that our cost of production is less ; and most certainly if Germany and America are ever able to take their duties off, as some people think in time they may be able, it will be no day of rejoicing for us. For that would really mean that they were not afraid of us in their own home markets ; that by consequence they were stronger than ever in the neutral market ; and, worst of all, that they might seriously and 'fairly' threaten us in our home market— not with cheap cartel or trust produced goods dumped down on us while the prices abroad were maintained high, but goods produced more cheaply than we could produce them. And if they then improved something more, it would mean that the time had really arrived when *we* should have to think of protective duties to save our own home market for our own producers. But the day for such an inversion of parts—Germany or America becoming a free trade and England a protectionist nation—is happily distant. What will probably take place

will be a keen and prolonged struggle (which is
already begun) between the three or four competing nations—a struggle in which *each* will
enlarge its foreign trade, but more by tapping
new regions and sending different goods than by
capturing each other's trade, though there will
also be some of the latter ; and the result will
not be the ruin and exclusive defeat of any
one of them, but a division of the commercial
empire of the world, so enlarged as to give each
a fairly good share.   In this process England's
share will increase, but from the very nature of
the case not in the same proportion as that of
her competitors, whose share, fifty years ago, was
infinitesimal.

Even in the worst imaginable case, where we
took only the second or third place in the neutral
markets, without being wholly excluded, and
where Germany, suppose, grew rich partly at
our expense by annexing some of our markets, we
should recover some of that wealth so long as
Germany herself did *any* trade at all with us.   Of
these commodities that England produces, and
which are desired in Germany—and there is still
a considerable amount of such, as proved by the
exports of 1902, amounting to over 22,000,000*l.*
—she will buy more, so that while one class
of English producers and exporting merchants

would lose, another would gain. This comes from the fact that a country gains more in exchange with a rich than a poor country, for the former can afford to give more, and will give more, if, as we should expect, its desires increase in proportion to its wealth for these things it does not produce itself; and in this way a country might get back from her successful competitor a large part of what she had lost in the competitions in the neutral markets; and the more there was of free trade, the more she might hope to recover on these trades where she still had some superiority.

The loss of the neutral market would be serious for certain industries, and especially for the cotton, our greatest industry for export. If China, Japan, India, Egypt, Turkey, part of South America, no longer wanted our cottons it would be serious, almost ruinous, for Lancashire, so much of the manufacture depending on foreign consumption. But this is very unlikely to happen. The most that is to be feared is a diminution of the trade, as India and Japan themselves engage in the manufacture. America may produce more cotton goods, but for a long time yet will not be able to supply her own wants, much less compete with us, while the cotton exports of France and Germany are relatively small.

But, taking all our leading manufactures, the

worst we have to fear is a division of the field,
while with our great advantages which we still
hold, our capital, our ships, our undoubted skill, the
intelligence and energy of our captains of industry
(especially if we add to all this something that we
may learn from our rivals, just as they have learned
from us), we might reasonably hope to do much
more to maintain our supremacy, and especially as
against our two most formidable rivals, Germany
and the United States, the latter of which will
soon have enough to do to minister to the wants
of her own vast and increasing population.

We have a certain additional advantage over
all competitors in the markets of India and
Egypt, as we have in our colonies (even without
preferential tariffs) so far as they purchase manufactured goods ; and when all these advantages
are put together it may confidently be stated that,
apart from colonial preferences, our prospects are
fairer than those of any other nation, the United
States alone excepted ; while with the colonial
preferences and certain benefits that may be
secured through successful negotiations, we may
look forward to the future with still greater
confidence.

CHAPTER VI

MR. CHAMBERLAIN'S PROPOSALS

I

LET us now compare the conclusions we have reached with Mr. Chamberlain's proposals as outlined in his recent speeches, bearing in mind that the original object was to increase our contracting or stationary exports by a system of mutual preferences with the colonies, by which the colonies gave us a preference over our competitors, and perhaps in time would lower their tariffs in our favour, while we, in turn, placed a tax on imported food, from which the colonies' exports were exempted. With this was joined retaliation or negotiation, to prevent the diminution of our market in protected countries—such as Germany, France, or the United States—and especially to prevent the practice of dumping, with its possible evil effects on our industries. By these means Mr. Chamberlain thought that workers' wages would be raised, because more

labour would be required for the increased
exports, while employers' profits would also be
secured.   And as regards this part of his scheme,
we go largely with him, and. even on free trade
principles.

But we find in his later speeches that he aims
at a different and far larger thing : at an economically self-sufficient and self-contained Empire, and
that, as steps on the way to it, the comparatively
moderate and safe proposals of preferential tariffs
on corn, and retaliation in case of unfair or unequal treatment, are expanded into a. complete
system of protection to the manufactures of the
United Kingdom, and a much more extensive
system of preference to the agricultural interest
of the colonies.   The 2s. duty on corn (not high,
certainly) is supplemented by a 5 per cent. duty on
colonial meat, dairy produce, and wine, while an
average duty is put on imported manufactures of
10 per cent.   And, for the reasons already given,
we object to protection in case of our manufactures (except in certain specified cases, for special
reasons), and mainly because we believe that
free trade is still the best for us on the whole,
however it be with other countries.   The first
arrangement was intended to be for mutual benefit ;
and so far as concerns the tax on corn we accepted
it, having regard to such prospective mutual ad-

vantages. We do not accept the tax of 5 per cent. on meat and dairy produce, because it would raise the price of those necessaries to the working man, even allowing that his bread would escape.

Then we have a general tax on imported manufactures mainly intended for the benefit of the corresponding home manufactures in competition with them, and this includes semi-manufactured goods—such as leather, wood, unwrought iron, which are really materials for further manufacture in England—as well as chemicals, glass wares, machinery, iron, and steel. These taxes are to be partly for revenue purposes, or possibly as retaliatory taxes, but mainly for protective purposes; at any rate, they are to be universal and put on everything that, by the widest stretch of the word, can be called manufactures—oil, unwrought iron, leather.

To benefit the colonies and so tie them closer by material bonds, and at the same time to benefit the export trade, including our manufacturers and their labourers, was the object of the first—the preferential scheme; to benefit certain manufactures pressed close in competition by the Germans or Americans is the object of the second. Under the first scheme Mr. Chamberlain is a free trader; he uses free trade arguments, especially when he requires that the colonies shall not start 'unsuitable' industries in competition with suitable and successful ones existing in England, and again where he thinks it best for Canada to leave to England the manufactures and let her produce corn, meat, timber, and dairy produce.   In the second case, where he is anxious to save English industries, he is all in favour of a country being self-sustaining, producing as much as possible for herself—at least of manufactures.   He is quite away from the free trade view, which does not aim at making a country self-supporting; but, on the contrary, requires each country to produce only its *best* and draw on others for their best.

In his speech at Newcastle he is fully protectionist, and he says that our exports of manufactures have fallen by 86 millions as compared with 1872, and that half of that amount or more might have gone as wages to working men. 'We have lost 46 millions in wages' (the fall in exports is included), thus implying that the increase in the imports of manufactured goods is an immense loss to the working classes of England.

But, we must ask, Why did we import the goods?' The answer is that there was a demand in England for the goods, either because they were not produced in England—as in the case of oil or certain chemicals, iron, or leather; or they were better than those produced in England, or they were of a different variety and appealed to different classes of customers. As a rule, they were not produced in England at all. And why? Because our manufacturers had turned to the production of other things that they thought would be more profitable, such as cotton, or linen, or woollens, or lace, or hosiery, or machinery, etc. Had they been able to produce the imported things with advantage, or cheaper than other countries, some capitalists would have produced them. The reason they did not do so was because they saw more favourable fields of enterprise, and because the Germans had already started them and had all the trained labourers; so that if any individual employer or company had attempted it they would have had very great difficulties to contend with, and small chances of fair profits, as the Germans would have undersold them unless our Government, copying the German Government, had protected them during the struggling years. Even with protection the chances are against their success unless the duties are exclusive, which would be bad policy.

Had the industry indeed been one as respects which we had special advantages, the Government might, on Mill's principle of protecting promising infant industries, have granted protection, but adherence to the general principle of free trade forbade this; so our great capitalists or companies tried some other industry where there appeared as sure a demand and a less struggle. They turned to some of the staple industries already existing, or they started a new one in which they gave as much additional employment as they would have done had they attempted to compete with the Germans. There is thus no such supposed loss of annual millions as Mr. Chamberlain from his speech appears to think. Wherever there is the most effective demand our promoters and capitalists find it and cater for it, if possible. They employ the necessary labour, if it can be had, whether for bicycles, or motor cars, or electric apparatus; but sometimes it may be very difficult to find the trained labour in England, in which case they are likely to leave it to the foreigners, and with advantage to them and us.

This does not apply to some of the chemical, glass, tinplate, and other industries, that we once had as well as the Germans, but in which the latter undersold us. We were beaten for the most part in fair fight. We might indeed have put on a 20 per cent. duty and so have saved the

industries.   But we had adopted the principle of
free trade after a long debate, believing it to be
the best on the whole for us that the consumer
should be allowed to buy in the cheapest market,
which in these cases was the German market.
Free trade apart, it is a question of the balance
of evils.   If we had protected the industries the
consumer would have been taxed to benefit inert
or inferior producers, and made to pay higher
when as good or better commodities were to be
had at a lower price.   It is a sad thing to see
workers driven out of employ, and employers
losing their sunk capital ; but there would be
greater evil if protection became general.   Besides,
the evil is really not quite so great.   The dismissed workers in the glass industry at Tyne-
mouth (suppose) go to London or some other
place, where other varieties of glass manufacture
are still carried on successfully.   The tinplate trade,
after temporary depression from high American
duties, has found other markets, and again
flourishes.   The cases where a large industry
has been wholly ruined are rare indeed, and
where it has happened, as it may sometimes in
a free trade country that invites foreign competition, it is a case of 'survival of the fittest,' and
the result of the general application of a principle
believed to be good on the whole for England.   It

produces some evils ; but if the opposite system, protection, became general it would produce still greater evils.   It would encourage routine, taking things easy ; it would raise prices generally without raising wages, or, to express it otherwise, it tends to make a country generally the poorer ; while in our days there is a new objection to it that it greatly facilitates the growth of great monopolies (Trusts and Cartels,) by which a second and probably larger tax, in addition to the protective tax, is levied on the consumer.

In Mr. Chamberlain's argument it is supposed that the labourers in general are injured by any imported manufactures that English labourers might have made.   But this is not the case.   It is not the free trade view, which is that the English labourers are better employed elsewhere.   They are employed in making the exports which make possible the purchase of these imported manufactures, and which is the cheapest and easiest way of getting them.   We did not make them, because we were making the exported things in which we had an advantage. We probably could have made both, but we dropped some branches of some industries and did not start others because we could do better.   If we tried to make *both*—the imports where others excel us, and the exports where we excel others—we should have to make less of the latter, because there will be less imports to be set against them ; and, secondly, we should be wasting a good part of our labour in making the imports.

It is well, therefore, that there are some imported manufactures, if there is any advantage in an international division of labour, and if it is possible for some foreign nations to manufacture some things better than we, and profitable for us to buy these or get them in exchange. The opposite view comes from the belief that we ought to make everything for ourselves ; that it is good to do so even though others could make many things at less price and with less labour, and can make some things we cannot make at all. Hence the belief that whatever manufactures are imported is a loss, and especially to the working classes because they exclude them from work that they might have done.

II

It all comes from one root, that it is best to produce everything for ourselves, thus surrendering all the advantages of foreign trade. It is the notion of the self-sustained, self-sufficing State that is at the bottom of this, and as there is a certain limited truth in the theory of the self-sustained State, it becomes all the more plausible as an ideal in the case of the British Empire, which, of course, is far more self-sufficing than the United Kingdom.   But it is not a true ideal, and least of all for England, which gains more than any nation from her imports of food, raw materials, and even manufactured goods.

Moreover, if the ideal of a self-sufficient empire be aimed at, a great deal further taxation will be necessary.   For the taxation of raw materials would have to be included, because some sort of raw materials for our numerous industries—cotton, woollen, linen, silk, iron, furniture, shipbuilding, house-building, etc.—do exist and could be procured within the Empire, however inferior in kind or limited in quantity some might be ; and it would be necessary, so as to give the preference to our own, to shut out by taxes the better materials procurable elsewhere, whether raw cotton, wool, silk, timber, leather, iron, etc.   And such taxes, besides raising the prices of the finished inferior articles on the consumer within the Empire, would speedily exclude us from the neutral market, where we are closely pressed by competitors (as well as from the protected foreign market).   In both cases, in consequence of the rise of price, we should be undersold and we should lose an export trade of far larger value than that with all the colonies and India, the former trade amounting in 1902 to 170,000,000*l.* as compared with 107,000,000*l.* worth of goods sent to the latter ; and this latter only admits of a slow increase in the case of the colonies.

This would mean the ruin, first of Lancashire, more than one-half of whose vast exports is sent to protected countries and neutral markets. The cotton manufacturers (spinners and weavers) have already protested against even the smallest rise in the price of the raw materials, pressed as they are so closely in competition by their protected rivals. The woollen and worsted industry, so far as it produces for export, would suffer still more, as the chief foreign purchasers are in protected countries or in neutral markets, in proof of which it was recently asserted on behalf of the woollen trade 'that the taxation of foreign wool would be disastrous to important branches of the woollen industries.' In like manner, the taxation of imported raw flax would seriously handicap the linen industry of Ulster, the principal exports of which are to protected countries, such as the United States. In the iron and steel and other metal trades it is the same story. The protected countries and the neutral market take fully two-thirds of the

H

exports, the value of which is second only to that
of cotton.   All these great industries, except the
woollen, produce mainly for the foreign market,
whether protected or neutral, and that they would
not find a sufficient one in the colonies, India,
and the home market is evident, not to speak of
the special difficulty that the colonies (Canada
and Victoria) are striving their best to keep us
out of their markets by high protective duties on
the products of the above industries.

There are many other industries which depend
on cheap materials sent from abroad—materials
such as timber, leather, jute, iron ore or part-
manufactured iron—and where afterwards the
finished product is exported in the shape of ships,
machinery, etc., and in these cases we should
either be beaten by competitors or lose part of
the market by too high prices.

No statesman could contemplate with equa-
nimity such disastrous losses of trade, and Mr.
Chamberlain must therefore say, as I believe he
has said, that he does not propose to put any tax
on materials, but only on manufactures (though
there are important classes of commodities that
are both materials and partly manufactured goods),
the first for the benefit of the colonies, the
second for the benefit of our own employers and
labourers, by assuring to them the home market

through the 10 per cent. duty. And the full reply
is, that while the colonies will certainly be benefited, the price of the food of the people will
certainly be raised, even though bread may not,
owing to the smallness of the duty; that the
taxes on imported manufactures will do as much
harm as good, to say the very least, by raising
prices and encouraging and propping up inefficient producers; finally, that if there is no
tax put upon imported materials, as well as imported manufactures, Mr. Chamberlain must be
content with very slow progress to the self-
sustaining empire.

In short, the dilemma is this : If you tax
materials you lose three-quarters of your markets
by being beaten by close competitors, or by shutting off the demand, even where there are no
competitors; if you do not, you get no nearer to
the self-sufficient empire, while you raise the price
of all food (bread and bacon excepted), and a
good many manufactured articles. And the latter
result, I think, will prove very unpalatable to the
working classes, unless you can offer them something in return more substantial than colonial
preferences, which still require high protective
walls against our manufactures.

Of course in a world-wide Empire containing,
as Mr. Chamberlain truly affirms, all kinds of

H 2

raw materials for necessaries, conveniences, and most luxuries, there need be no want of remunerative labour, for the poor in one part of the Empire might remove to another, where they would be sure to find employment and wages. But they can do so now, however small the comfort is in many cases. There is employment in Canada and Australia for many kinds of labourers. Would they be any better under the self-sustaining empire? They would then only move within its bounds; at present they often go to the United States. But, as within the self-contained empire there would be exclusive taxes put on all raw materials, food, and manufactures produced outside it, the probability is that there would be less work than at present, that many trades would expire that depended on materials and half-manufactured commodities obtained outside the Empire; in any case, that labourers and employers would have to work harder for less reward, than at present under an Empire which happily is not self-contained. Cheap raw materials and cheap competing commodities will be kept out, and the numerous smaller luxuries at present accessible to people of moderate means, and even to the working classes, will be excluded in order to encourage the production of however poor a substitute within the Empire.

There are very desirable things outside the British Empire ; wine and oil, and spices, and silks, and costly fabrics, and many manufactured goods, rare and choice commodities for wealthy people that we do not make ; and if we shut out in Chinese fashion all foreign luxuries, we simply render a great part of the wealth of rich people useless to them, in which case rich employers will hardly be likely to plan and labour ceaselessly and effectively to make more money with which they could do little, and whose real value or purchasing power would be so depreciated. They could only purchase things within the Empire, unless the stringency of these virtually sumptuary laws were relaxed and the high tariff on choice foreign productions reduced.

I incline to think there would be a paralysis of energy in the economic field, listless labourers, a want of heart and hope, a diminution of effort on the part of employers, and a less keen search for new methods on the part of inventors, even admitting a rude plenty of the commoner necessaries and comforts of life. Industrial stagnation and retrogression would in all human probability be the result in a self-contained empire, without the healthy rivalry so bracing to the faculties which competition with other nations ensures.

The truth is that it is only as a step towards

a self-contained empire (itself but a step to some form of Imperial Federation) that these taxes on food and manufactures were ever thought of. And if the scheme went no further in the direction of the goal aimed at, the total good would appear so dubious and small at best that no statesman would propose, in order to get it, such a serious thing as a complete reversal of the fiscal policy, under which it is clear that we have prospered to a wonderful extent and which has therefore all the presumptions in its favour ; on the other hand, if he does press further on, as is the undoubted aim, a tax on materials and an increased tax on imported manufactures will be necessary. This would be an undoubted step towards the self-sufficient empire ; but the faster this policy is pursued and the nearer we come to the end, the quicker and fuller will be the decline and final ruin of our industrial supremacy in the foreign protected and neutral markets ; and with it the ruin of the industries themselves.

The conclusion to be drawn is that the self-sufficing empire is not a good ideal so long as we are engaged in a great and necessary world-wide commercial struggle ; it would only become so as a *dernier ressort*, on a supposition not likely to be realised, that we shall be beaten hopelessly in the neutral markets—a supposition that will never be realised unless we are a people declining in energy, enterprise, and intelligence, and failing to secure the success which is their natural result, of which there are as yet no signs but the contrary. It is an ideal that happily can wait, and with it the system of taxation formed solely with reference to it, and which in itself is not to be recommended except in so far as part of it may fall under the head of equitable retaliation against unfair foreign duties.

The natural genesis of the notion of a self-contained empire is not difficult to see. The colonial trade has been increasing. It might be further increased by giving the colonies a preference in our markets. In time they could produce for us all the food and raw materials we require, and as they grow more populous they will want our manufactures. Unfortunately they are starting manufactures for themselves, but happily it might be arranged in a friendly way, if they would only agree not to start any new ones in competition with ours. The existing ones will not grow at the rate of the English ones, or perhaps competition between them can be merged in some such way as it now is in the United States, by some form of amalgamation, which would be easy if foreign competition were excluded.

On the other hand the trade with foreign

protected countries, the United States, France, and Germany, is falling off; while these same countries are invading and occupying our markets. We are forced by their exclusion to rely more on our colonies. Let us keep the foreigners out by a 10 per cent. duty in the meantime. This will be a drag on them, and it can easily be raised to the prohibitive point, following their own example, and especially that of the United States. By this means we can shut out their goods and thus be compelled or induced to produce them for ourselves. And in this way we go forward to the great goal of an economically self-sustaining and self-sufficient empire, united at first commercially and at length politically, independent of all the world and regardless of other civilised countries.

Such is the natural evolution of the ideal. The weakness lies in the fact that what is desired from the point of view of the United Kingdom—namely, expansive exports, so necessary for the sale of our wares and the employment of our population—is incompatible with a self-contained empire which requires no foreign trade—no trade outside its borders except such a small amount as would suffice to supply the few foreign luxuries that might be allowed to enter.

England is still, happily, the richest country in the world, the United States perhaps excepted.

She is still the envy of the world, her ships crowding every sea, her tonnage equalling the rest of the world put together. Small as she is in area, the marvel is that she is still the greatest manufacturing, commercial, and carrying power. As part of a self-contained empire, the dazzling vision of the Imperial federationist, she would soon cease to be the greatest commercial power. Her trade being limited to the colonies and India, and her neutral market and continental market gone, her great function as the world's carrier would cease—she would no longer be employed. Her present vast tribute from all nations, which now enables thousands to live in opulence without effort, would in time melt and could not be replaced owing to the drying up of the present overflowing spring of ever-increasing capital and the contraction of her commerce. Britannia would no longer be the mistress of the seas, however she might, for a time, with her warships 'rule the waves.' But it would not be for long time, as the attainment of the self-sufficient empire would be the beginning of her decline and fall.

And then let us consider that the immediate first step on the road to this Empire is by a system of duties which, at the lowest estimate, will raise the price of certain necessaries of the working

classes, as they cannot all be pushed back on the
producer; which will raise the price of some
materials of manufacture even at once ; which will
raise therefore the price of the manufactured
goods and check exports ; that the proposed tax
on manufactures will act on prices and credit
and trade generally in ways that we can scarcely
follow, but which would have great effects in
the total. If the tax largely stopped imports
the balance of trade would be disturbed, and a
greater balance would be due to us ; which
would cause in time an elevation of prices which,
again, would produce further effects. Every part
of the delicate and sensitive economic and financial
structure would be powerfully affected, and not
temporarily. Credit would be contracted, capital
timid, new enterprise and invention discouraged,
by the fear of the unknown. There would be
paralysis of trade and depression, with the certain
accompaniment of an increased multitude out of
employment ; because it is not a small matter or
one thing at a time that is proposed—it is a
revolution in our fiscal system. And before things
could settle and adjust themselves to the new
situation there would be the prospect of further
changes and more duties, a further rise of prices,
higher duties on materials, which would be necessary to reach to the goal of the self-contained

empire; a fresh series of disturbances of all trades, markets, and foreign exchanges.

Chambers of commerce, bankers, and financiers from past experience might make some attempt at calculating the likely consequences. But the calculation would fall short of the reality, and we should in all human probability be confronted early on the road to the Empire with the sobering fact of a distressed and hungry people. Therefore, if our Government must do a rash and perilous thing by the mandate of the people, if it must take a leap into unknown dangers—that are only unknown as to kind and amount, but well known in their general nature—let it take only one step at a time and see the effect, so as to allow of a possible retreat in case of need.

If indeed our great staple industries, the textile, the iron and steel, machine making, etc., ever became seriously threatened in the home market, from necessity we should be obliged to protect them in order to save the home market at least; though such protection would be of no avail in the neutral markets, nor yet in the protected foreign markets, which would no longer need protection against us. On the day, indeed, that we need such protection we are a declining if not a doomed nation, and it is then, and only then, that Mr. Chamberlain's scheme would be the sole way of salva-

tion that would remain. For if we were beaten
in the struggle in the neutral market, it would be
necessary to retain by protection the home market
for our own producers, and the colonial and Indian
markets by preferences; and after vast disloca-
tions of industry and privations and colossal
losses of capital we might recover and do passably
as part of a self-sufficient empire, provided our
colonies and India would prefer our manufactures
rather than their own.

Now it is just possible that that day may come.
But happily it has not yet come, nor is it at all
threateningly near. Our exports in our great
industries show no sign of decline in 1902, nor
for the first nine months of the past year. Nor
has the day arrived when we need dread fair competition in our markets in certain branches of
these same industries, nor in any save minor
industries.

We are still first in the neutral market; we
are still the richest nation; our labourers are
better paid than the labourers in France or
Germany; they have at least as constant employment and less working hours per day.

The present is certainly not the time to begin
a fiscal revolution that may be necessary some
fifty years hence if the industrial lead in our
main manufactures be taken from us, though it

may be a proper time to see that our rivals deal fairly with us.

But, it is said, it will be too late fifty years or twenty years hence; it will not do to postpone matters at all. We shall not be able to have a commercially united empire if we delay longer, and the union that could alone save us will then be impossible. For the colonies will have parted from us if we do not bind them to us now, if we do not embrace the opportunity now offered by them. To which it may be replied that a limited preferential treatment is all that is now desirable in view of future chances, and that it would be very unwise to introduce a complete fiscal revolution in view of what never may be necessary, and will be necessary only in case we are generally and hopelessly beaten in the international industrial struggle, while the revolutionary measures proposed would, in the struggle that lies immediately before us, hopelessly handicap us and ensure our early defeat and retirement from the field. For so sure as we make the self-sufficient empire our immediate aim we shall be forced to extend the fiscal scheme to raw materials and we shall be beaten in the general competition; our vast commerce in the neutral markets, that we might easily retain and increase, we shall lose in pursuit of largely illusory gains.

It remains to be seen whether the people will sanction the proposed scheme.   Mr. Chamberlain is indeed a very influential man with the working classes and people of England generally.   He is our most prominent man, and a very able and a very courageous man.   He is, further, a patriotic man, whose sincerity no one doubts. He may carry the people with him, though I have some doubts about it.   But I have no doubt that, if he does carry them with him and they go the whole way, it will bring disaster in its train, and that if ever they find themselves within the self-sustained empire they will be far from satisfied with it.   I do not, however, imagine the people of England will ever really experience the disasters signalled above, because long before we get to the goal the evils will be so pronounced and manifest that it will be impossible to pursue the scheme further.   I expect that the scheme will be modified and much of it dropped, so that little will remain but a preferential tax on corn and an equitable scheme of reciprocity, or, that failing, of retaliation.   I may be wrong in this anticipation, and I now go on to show a still deeper objection to the theory of the self-sufficient empire.

CHAPTER VII

IMPERIAL FEDERATION

ACCORDING to Mr. Chamberlain, the self-contained empire is only a means to an end, and that end is a grand empire united politically as well as economically. It is as a means to the 'greatest empire that the world has yet seen' that both his present scheme of tariffs and his hoped-for self-sustained empire are to be regarded. A political union and a great empire, one and undivisible, is the final goal; and apparently from his recent speeches, were there any other possible and better means, he is ready to adopt them. He has challenged his opponents to produce a better plan for a political union. He has stated that he had thought of other proposals, such as an Imperial Council, but that it was declared by the colonial premiers to be premature; that he had thought of an Imperial Zollverein, but found difficulties in the way such as the existing protective tariffs in the colonies;

and that there seemed no other course open save preferential treatment on both sides, which has been developed into the completely protective scheme whose merits we have just considered.

The mother idea of the whole was the vision of a great British Empire united politically, but far more closely and indissolubly than the existing British Empire, which is tied together by mere gossamer threads, and so lightly that the colonies might easily drift away as they grow stronger. They have the power to do so if they have the desire. They can go away and become separate states, and they will do so unless we bind them by ties of interest as well as of sentiment. Hence the preferential scheme and the notion of mutual dependence economically, and the exclusion of foreign productions by tariffs. But the political union requires more. There must be some kind of a federal union, for what else does Imperial Federation imply? And it was as the only means to this end that the whole proposals were made. We have examined these means and found them undesirable, now let us examine the end itself—a grand Imperial Federation. It will be found not unprofitable and will furnish additional reasons against Mr. Chamberlain's proposals and others similar.

Let us first regard the existing state of things. We have a great British Empire at present, of which the colonies form important and growing parts. They are practically independent, and they are contented at present. The unity of the Empire depends in the last resort on the supremacy of the Imperial Parliament, and the moral or sentimental bond of a desire for the connection. The system works well because it has been the policy of the Imperial Government to interfere with the internal affairs of the colonies as little as possible. As Professor Dicey says, under this system there has been little friction, because there has been so much freedom. All things point to leaving the existing system alone, and whenever the colonies ask for further autonomy, to grant it; as they now appear to wish for the treaty-making powers in regard to matters where they are even more concerned than the Imperial Government. At present the great colonies are in training for the responsibilities and dignity of states, should they ever wish to become independent. Leave them alone, and give them more freedom if they ask for it. The reason any considerable change would be undesirable is that it is not possible at present to foresee what would be best for them and for us, and a premature federation, made when they were in a comparative state of inexperience, would only tie their future will. It is very unlikely that they would consent to any scheme that could be devised at present. All their past history and all their present autonomy are unfitting them for any scheme of federalism, unless the word is used as an empty metaphor without its usual meaning, or unless a new kind of federalism be devised without the nature and essence of federalism.

A premature federalism would suit neither them nor England at present. They would fret under the fetters of a federal system or constitution or pact, and it would prove abortive speedily. But even if the colonies accepted such—after having enjoyed so great autonomy, if they put themselves under the necessary limitations of federalism—still, when they had grown to be great communities of twenty millions, would they be likely to remain content with the system?

At present they have liberty, they have their own special problems to work out, and they have their own special environment. Give them amplest freedom, which is their right, in order to work out their own destiny. Do not bind them in a federal constitution which would hinder their freedom of action, which would lead to jars and friction, and which would finally prove intolerable to us not less than to them ; and that all these evil consequences would follow can be easily proved. It lies in the nature of federal institutions and constitutions, and in the present instance still more in the peculiar circumstances of the case, where the federation would embrace great states divided by thousands of miles, confronted by different problems, and having quite divergent interests. For federalism at its best is a weak government, and for a great state like England, which for a long time must be by far the most important member of such a federation, it would paralyse her arm, prevent the concentrated energy and singleness of will, that is necessary in great crises, and where to be weak or fettered might mean ruin. It would necessarily destroy the supremacy of our Parliament, because it would imply a federal constitution, as in the United States, and in such case the House of Commons would no longer be supreme. We should have a brand-new chamber at Westminster, with representatives from the colonies in proportion to their population, and a new constitution supplanting our historic constitution, the growth of centuries. The action of this central chamber would be weakened, because its hands would be tied by the federal pact or constitution, and the possibility of divergent views between the representatives of the United Kingdom and the colonies, and the friction would be likely to increase as the colonies grew stronger.

It would be most unsatisfactory to the colonists; it would be ruinous to England. At present the colonies do not feel their wishes thwarted, there being so little restraint. They are 'self-governing'; they have full Home Rule. There is only a faint possibility of restraint, which has grown less and less. Change this state of things which works so well, and set a new constitution over their heads and over our heads, instead of the British Parliament, which is the expression of our Will, and which knows no restraint, except constitutional usage, or common morality, and you increase greatly the possibility of disagreement. It would become a daily sore, and the simplest way to cure it would be to restore the *status quo* and dissolve the federal pact; and it might go farther. We, on our side, would certainly, under the circumstances, be glad to do the former. But it might be too late. The colonies might take the opportunity to assert their complete independence, and we should certainly use no force to prevent them.

We should be glad to restore the old system after a painful experience; would it not then be better not to make such a federal pact which would weaken the hands of the predominant

state, and for a mere nominal and illusory
union of the parts in a greater whole, would
produce the very opposite thing? It would not
continue; it would lead either to a restoration of
the present system, or far more likely to complete separation.

It may be objected by the Imperial federationist, and especially by Mr. Chamberlain, that
he contemplates no such scheme, and has not
committed himself to any definite plan. The
reply is that what I have stated above is federalism over the world and through all history.
It contains the essence of all possible federalism,
and any less kind of federalism would be open
to similar objections, though less the further it
departs from full federalism. Of course, if the
scheme does not go so far—that is, if it does not
much depart from our present nominal federalism
with merely moral and sentimental bonds—there
would be less objection, but only because it leaves
a system which has the maximum of liberty to
each of the parts which are all but Sovereign
States.

And it is clear enough that both Mr.
Chamberlain and Lord Rosebery have been for
some years past in quest of a new recipe for a
federal union not open to the above objections.
But they have neither of them yet struck on it,

though they have both vaunted the grandeur of
Imperial Union and Imperial Federation without
showing us how to attain either the union or the
federation. The happy inspiration has not come
yet to either. For it is an extremely difficult
problem how to get to a closer union, while the
possibility of a true and real Imperial federation is
very far distant, even if it be ever possible. Much
better, therefore, to drop the word federation and
keep to Imperial union.

As a step towards such, an Imperial Council
has been suggested; but the colonial premiers
wisely declined it as premature. A scheme for
common defence was also proposed; this, of
course, is a much smaller thing, but there has been
no agreement as yet on the matter. The next
idea was a Zollverein. But that would not conduce
to a closer union; some of the manufacturers in
Canada and Australia being more inclined to raise
tariffs than to lower them. The latest idea is
preferential treatment, and the shutting out of all
the world by tariffs, by which it is thought that
the colonies and the mother country must perforce from material necessities come to a closer
union, but the result of which, as we have seen,
would probably be just the opposite.

The words of the colonial premiers that an
Imperial Council was ' premature ' were wise, and

indicate a right perception of the essential
nature of the problem of federation, and the true
method of dealing with it. The word 'premature'
implies that the time was not ripe for such an
innovation in our government and those of the
colonies.

The word implies that time is of the essence of
the problem, and that the time was not ripe for
such a step in the direction of federation, still less
for full federation. The problem is one to which
time and the experience it brings can alone furnish the answer, and that only in partial fashion,
and by no means all at once. As time goes on,
certain necessities or advantages will compel a
certain course. Special exigencies may be met by
devices suitable if a favourable occasion or con-
juncture of events presents itself. A statesman
may then 'take Occasion by the hand,' and more
may be done; but the manner will depend on
circumstances which the wisest cannot now foresee. Anyone regarding the course of history
can see that it is subject to chance as well as
evolution, and that things most unlikely and
unpredictable have taken place. And future
history will have the like surprises. The true
course for statesmen, therefore, is to wait on, and
not to force, events; to gather the will and desire
of the colonies; to wait still to see if the will is

permanent; and to do so in each case separately
as, being in different situations and different
stages of development, the colonies may not all
feel alike; above all, to defer taking decisive
steps till they are grown greater and wiser, that
they may be 'of age' before we invite them to
take steps having such momentous consequences
for good or ill.   Our statesmen may thus slowly
evoke so strong a desire for a more intimate connection that after a time there may no longer be a
desire for a completely separate political existence,
and it is even possible that a desire for some looser
kind of Imperial Federation might result.   Such
desire might be strengthened by the golden link
of the Crown ; our King is their King, and he is
very popular.   The office also is popular.   That
a king might do much to strengthen the sentimental bond, which is a far stronger one than
any material one can be, may be inferred from
the unsuspected depths of loyalty to the Crown
that was manifested to the King's son not long
since.   Royal visits to the greater colonies, the
conferring of honours and dignities, the throwing
open of high careers in England to ambitious
aspirants from the colonies, would be all steps in
the right direction, as would be likewise the proposed preferences duly limited between England
and the colonies.   All these, joined to a policy of

waiting and watching for opportunities for a closer political union, may bring us nearer to it. But for reasons already referred to I am inclined to believe that the union can never be so intimate as the federal union in America, nor is it desirable that it should be so, though the moral and sentimental bond might well be quite as complete.

To conclude. The only fatal policy is to attempt to anticipate and force the future by premature institutions or policies which in all probability would have exactly the opposite effect to that intended. The Empire as it stands is not at all in a bad condition ; it can afford to wait, and can endure with benefit a good deal of 'letting alone.'

PRINTED BY
SPOTTISWOODE AND CO. LTD., NEW-STREET SQUARE
LONDON

K

For Product Safety Concerns and Information please contact our EU
representative GPSR@taylorandfrancis.com
Taylor & Francis Verlag GmbH, Kaufingerstraße 24, 80331 München, Germany

www.ingramcontent.com/pod-product-compliance
Lightning Source LLC
Chambersburg PA
CBHW050718280326
41926CB00088B/3202

9 780367 246105